Norwich City Football Club
Official Yearbook 2005-06

Editorial
Peter Rogers, Marc Fiszman, Mark Peters

Design
Teb Scott, Simon Sharville, Ian Bull

Statistics
Karim Biria

Photography
Action Images

Copyright © 2005 Norwich City Football Club

Sidan Press, 63-64 Margaret St, London W1W 8SW
Tel: 020 7580 0200
Email: info@sidanpress.com

sidanpress.com

Club Directory

Norwich City Football Club, Carrow Road, Norwich NR1 1JE
Tel: 01603 760760 www.canaries.co.uk

Vice Presidents
Gavin Paterson, Barry Lockwood

Chairman
Roger Munby

Vice Chairman
Barry Skipper

Directors
Delia Smith, Michael Wynn Jones,
Michael Foulger

Chief Executive
Neil Doncaster

Football Manager
Nigel Worthington

Assistant Manager
Doug Livermore

First Team Coach
Steve Foley

Reserve Team Coach
Keith Webb

Goalkeeping Coach
James Hollman

Chief Scout
Alan Wood

Youth Development Officer
Colin Watts

Academy Manager
Ricky Martin

Youth Team Coach/Technical Director
David Williams

Physiotherapists
Neal Reynolds MCSP, Peter Shaw MCSP

Sports Scientist
Dave Carolan

Club Doctor
Dr Peter Harvey

Club Secretary
Kevan Platt

Director of Finance & Operations
Shaun O'Hara

Director of Sales & Marketing
Andrew Cullen

Head of Media
Joe Ferrari

Customer Services Manager
Richard Gough

Sponsorship Sales Manager
Bryan Gunn

Brand Marketing Manager
Will Hoy

Stadium Operations Manager
Leon Blackburn

General Catering Manager
Roland Schreiber

Programme Editor
Peter Rogers

Contents

The ball is in your half...

The choice is yours. Choose from our selection of stunning
new and pre owned Lotus Elise and Exige from one of our official UK
dealers who will be pleased to show you the cars and provide you with
all of the information you need to make your choice.

All of our pre owned cars sold within our official network have been HPI
checked to give you full peace of mind when purchasing your car.

The new Lotus Elise 111R is available from £28,705.00 OTR and the new
Lotus Exige can be yours from £30,705.00 OTR.

Call 0870 9000 565, email cars@lotuscars.co.uk or visit
www.lotuscars.co.uk today for details of your nearest official UK dealer.

www.lotuscars.co.uk   *Change the rules*

Chairman's Message

In your last yearbook it was my privilege to welcome you to the Premiership and congratulate you on the role that you, our fans, played in supporting your club. I was able to reflect on the spirit of togetherness and your positive support and suggested that one thing would be certain... that whatever happened in 2004-05, the Club would progress. And indeed, despite the fact that the season would ultimately end in disappointment, I do believe that we most certainly have progressed in the past 12 months.

There is no doubt that the spirit and behaviour exhibited by Nigel, his staff and the players – even in adversity – won many admirers throughout the world of football. Against the odds, seemingly doomed in March, our players took their fight right to the wire playing their part in one of the most extraordinary climaxes ever to a Premiership season. And who will ever forgot the exhilaration of victory against Manchester United and those nail-biting moments at home to Charlton and Birmingham, or the extraordinary scenes at the end of our home matches with Middlesbrough and Newcastle? The whole experience has made everyone stronger, hungrier and determined to succeed in the competitive season that lies ahead.

Off the pitch, you, our supporters, played your part, taking the number of sell-out games to 65 out of the last 70 to be played at Carrow Road. Away from home our travelling support was among the highest in the Premiership, setting new attendance records at Old Trafford, The Valley and The Riverside.

And for this season we must thank you for your magnificent response in purchasing a record 20,200 season tickets, ensuring that every game this season will once again be a home sell-out.

That volume of spirit will be important as we look ahead to taking our place in what we expect to be an extremely competitive Championship. Your Board's policy of prudence with ambition means that relegation need not spell the financial disaster it has sometimes meant for other clubs who have experienced relegation from the Premier League. Instead, there is no reason why we cannot aspire to the model set by Charlton and Bolton – and now, of course, West Bromwich Albion – who all recovered from relegation to consolidate their place in the Premier League.

Our coaching and management staff know the Coca-Cola Championship well and realise what is needed to successfully compete at the top of this division. The Board also understands that the Coca-Cola Championship is a competitive league and that we have no divine right to promotion. But we do believe that we are well-equipped and as determined as any other team to succeed in this division.

I would like to express the Club's thanks to those players who have left us over the summer. Phil Mulryne, Marc Edworthy, Gary Holt and Mathias Svensson all made special individual contributions to not only our promotion season in 2003-04, but to the special spirit of togetherness that exists throughout the Club. Along with Danny Crow, Thomas Helveg and Graham Stuart, we wish them well in their careers.

In conclusion, I am only too pleased to reiterate that our ambition remains solely focused on returning to the Premier League and competing there on a regular basis. I can assure you that while relegation is a setback, it does not represent a crisis for Norwich City Football Club.

We can look forward with much optimism to a very positive and secure future for the Club. This summer has been one of graft and hard work as we prepare for the season ahead. The Board is determined to do everything it possibly can, within its policy of prudence with ambition, to achieve early promotion back to the Premier League.

On the Ball City!

Roger Munby
Chairman

Control Freak

The new Proton GEN-2

With Lotus-tuned suspension you can handle anything life throws at you

For further information, call

0800 0 521 521

Alternatively, visit our website on

www.proton.co.uk

LOTUS DESIGN

Power & Control

Manager's Message

Although last season ended in disappointment with a heavy defeat and relegation from the Premier League, when I reflect upon the season as a whole I thought it was a wonderful experience for everyone associated with Norwich City Football Club.

There is no doubting that the Barclays Premiership is the place to be, and having had a taste of what it's all about, we will be doing all we can to get back there as soon as possible. Taking on some of the very best players in the world every week was a great challenge, and full credit must go to our players for keeping the season alive right until that final day.

I really feel that everyone at the Club came through last season with a great deal of credit. Our supporters were outstanding at every game and throughout the campaign we all stuck together as the Club gave a great account of itself both on and off the pitch. A number of our matches produced a great deal of goals and excitement and I felt the players' never-say-die attitude served them well throughout the season.

The most important thing we have gained from last season is experience. I feel that all the players and staff have benefited from the Premier League experience and we are a better and stronger group for it.

A number of players have left the Football Club over the summer and we wish them all well wherever their careers may take them. I'm hopeful that by the time you read this column we will have been able to bring in some new players of our own to compliment our existing group and increase competition for places during the coming season. I find myself penning these notes in early June and even though pre-season training is still almost a month away a great deal is going on behind the scenes to ensure the squad is up to the challenge come the big kick-off on Saturday, August 6, 2005.

The Coca-Cola Championship is an extremely tough league to get out of and there will be a good number of sides with realistic promotion ambitions this season. There are, of course, some big clubs in the division, but no one has any automatic right to promotion. Success on the pitch this season will need to come from hard work and everyone pulling together in the same direction for what is best for Norwich City Football Club.

Away from first-team matters, we enjoyed another successful season within the Academy set-up. Under the new management team of Ricky Martin and David Williams we were delighted to see two more players come through the system to earn professional contracts in the shape of Danny Crow and Joe Lewis. Although Danny has since been released to enable him to further his career elsewhere, I am sure the experience that both players have gained from their time in the Academy will serve them well throughout their respective careers. With the Reserve side now playing in the Barclays Premiership Reserve League, we were also able to measure the development of a number of the Academy scholars at that level as well as playing them in the youth team.

Many thanks for your support last season and please keep right behind us throughout the new season.

Nigel Worthington

Honours and Records

Year Formed: 1902
Turned Professional: 1905
Club Nickname: The Canaries

Previous Grounds

1902: Newmarket Road
1908-35: The Nest, Rosary Road
1935: Carrow Road

Football League Record

1920 Original member of Div 3; 1921 Div 3 (S);
1934-39 Div 2; 1946-60 Div 3; 1960-72 Div 2;
1972-74 Div 1; 1974-75 Div 2; 1975-81 Div 1;
1981-82 Div 2; 1982-85 Div 1; 1985-86 Div 2;
1986-1992 Div 1; 1992-95 Premier League;
1995-04 Div 1; 2004-2005 Premier League

League Honours

Premier League 3rd 1992-93
Division 1 Champions 2003-04
Division 2 Champions (2) 1971-72 & 1985-86
Division 3(S) Champions 1933-34
Division 3 Runners-up 1959-60
Division 1 Play-off finalists 2001-02

FA Cup

Semi-finalists 1959, 1989, 1992

Football League Cup

Winners 1962 & 1985; Runners-up 1973 &
1975

Record Attendance

43,984 vs Leicester City, FA Cup 6th Rd, March
1963

Record Receipts

£337,142 vs Wolverhampton Wanderers, Div 1
Play-off Semi-final, 1st leg, April 28, 2002

Managers Since 1946

Cyril Spiers; Doug Lochhead; Norman Low;
Tom Parker; Archie Macaulay; Willie Reid;
George Swindin; Ron Ashman; Lol Morgan;
Ron Saunders; John Bond; Ken Brown; Dave
Stringer; Mike Walker; John Deehan; Gary
Megson (caretaker); Martin O'Neill; Gary
Megson; Mike Walker; Bruce Rioch; Bryan
Hamilton; Nigel Worthington

Record Victories

League: 10-2 vs Coventry City, Div 3(S) March
1930
FA Cup: 8-0 vs Sutton United, 4th Rd, January
1989
League Cup: 7-1 vs Halifax Town, 4th Rd,
November 1963

Record Defeats

League: 0-7 vs Walsall, Div 3(S), September
1930;
0-7 vs Sheffield Wednesday, Div 3(S),
November 1938
FA Cup: 0-6 vs Luton Town, 2nd Rd,
December 1927;
0-6 vs Manchester City, 4th Rd, January 1981
League Cup: 1-6 vs Manchester City, 2nd Rd,
2nd Replay, September 1975

Most League Goals

99, Div 3(S) 1952-53

Most League Goals in a Season
Ralph Hunt (31), Div 3(S), 1955-56

League Sequence Records
Most matches undefeated
(20) Aug 31, 1950 - Dec 30, 1950

Most home matches undefeated
(12) Jan 31, 1970 - Sep 12, 1970

Most away matches undefeated
(12) Sep 14, 1985 - Feb 8, 1986

Longest run without a home win
(12) Sep 29, 1956 - Mar 2, 1957

Longest run without an away win
(41) Sep 3, 1977 - Aug 18, 1979

Most League wins
(10) Nov 23, 1985 - Jan 25, 1986

Most League defeats
(7) Sep 4, 1935 - Sep 28, 1935
& Jan 12, 1957 - Feb 23, 1957
& Apr 1, 1995 - May 6, 1995

Most League matches without a win
(25) Sep 22, 1956 - Feb 23, 1957

Most home wins
(12) Mar 15, 1952 - Sep 20, 1952

Most away wins
(5) Sep 3, 1988 - Nov 5, 1988

Record appearances
Kevin Keelan, 673
(571 Lge, 31 FAC, 57 FLC, 14 other)

Record League appearances
Ron Ashman, 592

Most goals in a career
Johnny Gavin 132 (122 Lge, 10 FAC)

Most goals in a match
Roy Hollis: 5 vs Walsall Div 3 (S), December 1951
Les Eyre: 5 vs Brighton & Hove Albion, FA Cup, November 1946

Most capped player
Mark Bowen (35 - Wales)

Oldest player
Albert Sturgess (42 yrs, 116 days)

Youngest player
Ryan Jarvis (16yrs, 282 days)

Record transfer fee received
£5million from Blackburn Rovers for Chris Sutton, July 1994; £5million from Coventry City for Craig Bellamy, August 2000

Record transfer fee paid
£3million to Crewe Alexandra for Dean Ashton, January 2005

Simon Charlton gets his body between Andy Johnson and the ball

Saturday, August 14, 2004 Type: **Premiership** Venue: **Carrow Road** Attendance: 23,717 Referee: P Walton

Norwich City 1-1 Crystal Palace

PREMIERSHIP FIXTURE HISTORY

	Pl: 3 Draws: 2	Wins ⚽	🟨	🟥
Norwich City	1	5	2	0
Crystal Palace	0	3	2	0

STARTING LINE-UPS

Green

Fleming Charlton

Helveg   Drury (c)

Francis Holt

Jonson   Bentley

Svensson Huckerby

Torghelle Johnson

Kolkka   Routledge

Hughes Hall

Granville   Boyce

Popovic (c) Hudson

Speroni

🟡 McVeigh,
Edworthy,
McKenzie,
Ward, Jarvis

🔴 Derry, Riihilahti,
Freedman, Kiraly,
Black

When Darren Huckerby hit his first Premiership goal for the newly-promoted Canaries, the home side looked odds on to collect all three points.

However, a spirited second-half Crystal Palace fightback brought an equaliser from Andrew Johnson, and in the end a draw was probably a fair result.

The visitors began brightly, with Emmerson Boyce and Wayne Routledge combining well down the right, but the home side were soon into their running, forcing three corners in quick succession.

The opening goal took just 16 minutes to arrive, Huckerby nudging Mark Hudson off the ball to collect Matthias Svensson's pass before advancing and beating Julian Speroni with a blistering shot across goal from an inside-right position.

In the 25th minute, Huckerby began his run just too soon and was flagged offside with only the 'keeper to beat. This situation was repeated three or four times throughout the game.

Debutant David Bentley, on a season-long loan from Arsenal, was playing a starring role for the Canaries. Having created first-half openings for both Huckerby and Simon Charlton, the youngster took less than a minute of the second period to provide Svensson with a headed chance from which he should have done better.

Damien Francis puts Aki Riihilahti under pressure

STATISTICS

Season	Fixture			Fixture	Season
10	10	Shots On Target		8	8
4	4	Shots Off Target		6	6
0	0	Hit Woodwork		0	0
8	8	Caught Offside		4	4
6	6	Corners		11	11
12	12	Fouls		16	16
46%	46%	Possession		54%	54%

EVENT LINE

16	⚽ Huckerby (Open Play)
	HALF TIME 1 - 0
58	🟨 Granville (Foul)
64	🔄 **Jonson (Off) McVeigh (On)**
71	🔄 **Bentley (Off) Edworthy (On)**
73	⚽ Johnson (Open Play)
78	🔄 Hall (Off) Riihilahti (On)
78	🔄 Kolkka (Off) Derry (On)
82	🔄 **Svensson (Off) McKenzie (On)**
89	🔄 Hughes (Off) Freedman (On)
	FULL TIME 1 - 1

LEAGUE STANDINGS

Position (pos before)	W	D	L	F	A	Pts
11 (-) Norwich C	0	1	0	1	1	1
7 (-) Crystal Palace	0	1	0	1	1	1

PREMIERSHIP MILESTONE

The attendance of 23,717 was a Premiership record at Carrow Road.

Robert Green then denied Hungarian Sandor Torghelle with a spectacular facial block after the striker had got clear of the home defence.

At that point the Eagles were playing as well as they had at any stage in the match, forcing Norwich into some desperate defending.

Huckerby was denied a second goal by Speroni's fingertips with half-an-hour left to play, but no home player was alert to the rebound.

With 73 minutes on the clock, Johnson continued where he had left off last season, netting a smartly taken equaliser.

The striker was picked out by the impressive Routledge, having run in behind the Norwich defence, and was able to beat Green with a quickly dispatched low effort.

Both sides pushed for a winner, Speroni clutching an 18-yard Huckerby volley before Green kept out a Johnson strike at the second attempt.

> **"Darren Huckerby showed today that he can do it in the Premiership."**
> **Nigel Worthington**

Season Review 04-05

Darren Huckerby outpaces Roy Keane

Saturday, August 21, 2004 Type: **Premiership** Venue: **Old Trafford** Attendance: **67,812** Referee: **N Barry**

Manchester United 2-1 Norwich City

PREMIERSHIP FIXTURE HISTORY

	Pl: 4	Draws: 1	Wins ⚽	🟨	🟥
Manchester United	3		6	1	0
Norwich City	0		3	2	0

STARTING LINE-UPS

Howard

Keane (c)   Silvestre

G.Neville   O'Shea

Miller   Djemba-Djemba

Bellion   Giggs

Smith   Scholes

Huckerby   Svensson

Bentley   Jonson

Holt   Francis

Drury (c)   Helveg

Charlton   Fleming

Green

🔴 P Neville, Richardson, Ronaldo, Carroll, Eagles

🟡 McVeigh, Doherty, McKenzie, Ward, Edworthy

Manchester United picked up their first points of the season with a less than convincing victory against a spirited Canary side at Old Trafford.

French winger David Bellion registered his side's first goal of the campaign in the opening period, before summer signing Alan Smith looked to have secured victory with a stunning second shortly after the interval. However, the Canaries hit back 15 minutes from time through substitute Paul McVeigh, as Sir Alex Ferguson's side stuttered past the winning post.

With several star names missing from the teamsheet, United began in fairly cautious fashion. Patience seemed to be the watchword, with half-chances for Smith, John O'Shea and Ryan Giggs representing the home team's best efforts.

In fact, it was the visitors who came closest in the opening half-hour, David Bentley almost breaking the crossbar with a 30-yard drive.

That let-off seemed to galvanise the Old Trafford side as they broke upfield to take the lead, a Giggs cross from the left flicked on by Smith for Bellion to turn home on 32 minutes.

The Frenchman was denied a second four minutes later, his crisp, low shot from the right corner of the penalty area turned behind by 'keeper Robert Green.

Gary Doherty shields the ball from Mikael Silvestre

If Bellion's goal was well-worked, Smith's first Premiership strike for United five minutes into the second period was brilliantly executed.

Gary Neville's deep cross from the right was met by a cushioned header from Giggs. Having controlled the ball on his chest with his back to goal, Smith swivelled before dispatching a 12-yard volley over his right shoulder and in off the far post.

Far from using the goal as a springboard to push on, United retreated and invited Norwich back into the game.

The Canaries duly obliged, McVeigh capitalising on hesitancy in the home defence to cut in from the right and beat Tim Howard with a low left-foot shot.

"We are disappointed we got nothing from the game. For 35 minutes in the second half, Old Trafford was quiet."

Nigel Worthington

Season Review 04-05

David Bentley celebrates reducing the deficit

Wednesday, August 25, 2004 Type: **Premiership** Venue: **St James' Park** Attendance: **51,574** Referee: **M Halsey**

Newcastle United 2-2 Norwich City

PREMIERSHIP FIXTURE HISTORY

	Pl: 3	Draws: 1	Wins ⚽	🟨	🟥
Newcastle United	2	8	2	0	
Norwich City	0	2	1	0	

STARTING LINE-UPS

Given

Carr · O'Brien · Hughes · Bernard

Dyer · Butt · Robert

Milner

Bellamy · Shearer (c)

Huckerby · Doherty

Bentley · Holt · Francis · McVeigh

Drury (c) · Charlton · Fleming · Edworthy

Green

🔲 Ameobi, Bowyer, Harper, Elliott, Kluivert, 🟡 Jonson, McKenzie, Ward, Helveg, Svensson

Newcastle's miserable start to the campaign continued as they squandered a two-goal lead at home to the Canaries.

The Magpies didn't win a Premiership match until October last season, a run that ultimately cost them a Champions League place.

Goals either side of half-time from ex-Canary Craig Bellamy and defender Aaron Hughes looked to have sealed the three points in this encounter, but strikes from David Bentley and Gary Doherty saw Nigel Worthington's side pick up a valuable away draw.

Sir Bobby Robson's men started brightly enough, Laurent Robert seeing a header harshly ruled out and James Milner fully stretching Robert Green in the visitors' goal.

At the other end, Darren Huckerby was a coat of paint away from opening the scoring after seeing off the challenge of Olivier Bernard.

It was Newcastle who broke the deadlock through a 40th-minute Bellamy goal, the Wales international steering home a deflected 12-yard effort after Alan Shearer had knocked down a cross from the right.

Hughes doubled the home side's advantage five minutes after the break, the versatile defender stooping to head home Robert's inswinging flag-kick from six yards.

Gary Doherty revels in his equalising goal

Perhaps the men in black and white were guilty of believing the game was won, as Norwich caught them cold with an almost instant response.

Two minutes after Hughes's goal, Bentley was left unchallenged to fire home a low, swerving 25-yard effort that Shay Given would have been disappointed to have conceded.

Good chances continued to go begging at both ends before the Canaries drew level in the 74th minute, Doherty – making his first start since arriving from Tottenham – reacting quickest to turn the ball home from close range after Given had denied Craig Fleming.

Far from sparking the Magpies back into life, the equaliser gave encouragement to the visitors. A spectacular long-range shot from Huckerby almost found the top corner, while a poor first touch was all that prevented substitute Leon McKenzie from netting the winner.

For the second successive home match the jeers that greeted the final whistle left no doubt as to what the Geordie public thought of what they had witnessed.

"We showed people what we could do at Old Trafford for 30 minutes, and today we have done it for 90 minutes."

Nigel Worthington

Adam Drury sends the ball forward

Saturday, August 28, 2004 Type: **Premiership** Venue: **Carrow Road** Attendance: **23,944** Referee: **G Poll**

Norwich City 1-4 Arsenal

PREMIERSHIP FIXTURE HISTORY

	Pl: **4** Draws: **3**		Wins ⚽	🟨	🟥
Norwich City	0	3	6	0	
Arsenal	1	6	5	0	

STARTING LINE-UPS

Green

Fleming   Charlton

Edworthy   Drury (c)

Francis   Holt

McVeigh   Jonson

Doherty   Huckerby

Henry (c)   Reyes

Pires   Ljungberg

Gilberto   Fabregas

Cole   Lauren

Toure   Hoyte

Lehmann

Safri, McKenzie, Svensson, Ward, Helveg

Edu, Bergkamp, Clichy, Almunia

Arsenal continued their mesmerising start to the season, handing out a footballing lesson to Nigel Worthington's Canaries.

Norwich didn't play badly, but were ripped apart at will by a side with confidence levels in the clouds. Youngster Justin Hoyte slotted in seamlessly alongside Kolo Toure at centre-back following an injury picked up by Pascal Cygan in the warm-up, as the Gunners demonstrated their growing strength in depth.

The game began with a flurry of corners at both ends, then settled into a rhythm of swift attacks from the visitors.

José Antonio Reyes and Thierry Henry both tested Robert Green before the two combined for the opening goal, Henry using his pace and trickery down the left to lay on a simple close-range tap-in for the Spaniard in the 22nd minute.

Referee Graham Poll angered the home fans on the half-hour after failing to dismiss Lauren for what appeared to be a blatant professional foul on Darren Huckerby.

Home frustrations intensified six minutes later when Henry doubled his side's advantage, the French striker netting with a bullet header from Freddie Ljungberg's clipped cross from the right.

Darren Huckerby shows his strength

STATISTICS

Season	Fixture 🏆		🔴 Fixture	Season
22	6	Shots On Target	15	46
17	0	Shots Off Target	3	18
1	0	Hit Woodwork	0	3
19	2	Caught Offside	1	7
21	4	Corners	10	29
60	15	Fouls	5	39
43%	38%	Possession	62%	60%

EVENT LINE

22 ⚽ Reyes (Open Play)

30 🟨 Lauren (Foul)

36 ⚽ Henry (Open Play)

40 ⚽ Pires (Open Play)

HALF TIME 0 - 3

46 🔄 Jonson (Off) Safri (On)

50 ⚽ **Huckerby (Penalty)**

63 🔄 McVeigh (Off) McKenzie (On)

73 🔄 Fabregas (Off) Edu (On)

73 🔄 Reyes (Off) Bergkamp (On)

82 🔄 **Doherty (Off) Svensson (On)**

83 🟨 **Safri (Foul)**

84 🔄 Pires (Off) Clichy (On)

90 ⚽ **Bergkamp (Open Play)**

FULL TIME 1 - 4

LEAGUE STANDINGS

Position (pos before)	W	D	L	F	A	Pts
17 (16) Norwich C	0	2	2	5	9	2
1 (1) Arsenal	4	0	0	16	5	12

PREMIERSHIP MILESTONE

Youssef Safri made his Premiership debut for Norwich.

By the 40th minute it was three, slack play in his own box from Norwich skipper Adam Drury seeing him pick-pocketed by Ljungberg, with Robert Pires clinically sweeping home the loose ball from 12 yards.

Credit must go to Nigel Worthington and his team, who never gave up and pulled a goal back in the 50th minute.

It was Huckerby, the catalyst for so much of his side's best attacking work, who tempted Hoyte into a challenge that resulted in the award of a penalty. The former Coventry frontman duly stepped up to send Jens Lehmann the wrong way from the spot.

The Canaries were flying, as Huckerby and midfielder Gary Holt both forced fine saves from Arsenal's German 'keeper, but they had their wings clipped in injury time.

Substitute Dennis Bergkamp finished off a pacy break with a rapier-like right-foot finish from 15 yards that swerved beyond the left hand of Green.

"Although it is always disappointing to lose, Arsenal are a different class, even from Manchester United and Newcastle."

Nigel Worthington

Season Review 04-05

Jermain Defoe can't find a way through

Sunday, September 12, 2004 Type: **Premiership** Venue: **White Hart Lane** Attendance: **36,095** Referee: **HM Webb**

Tottenham Hotspur 0-0 Norwich City

PREMIERSHIP FIXTURE HISTORY				
Pl: **4** Draws: **1**	Wins ⚽	🟨		🟥
Tottenham Hotspur	2	7	4	0
Norwich City	1	4	5	0

STARTING LINE-UPS

Robinson

Pamarot Naybet King Edman

Brown Redknapp (c) Mendes Atouba

Kanoute Defoe

Huckerby Doherty

Holt Bentley Francis

Drury (c) Safri Edworthy

Charlton Fleming

Green

🔲 Davies, Keane, Jackson, Keller, Gardner

🟢 McVeigh, McKenzie, Helveg, Ward, Svensson

Tottenham were denied by the heroics of Norwich 'keeper Robert Green as the sides played out a goalless draw at White Hart Lane.

Jacques Santini opted to pair Jermain Defoe with Fredi Kanoute in attack, while Norwich boss Nigel Worthington set his midfield out in a diamond formation. Youssef Safri was handed a first start following his summer move from Coventry and anchored a foursome that had Arsenal loanee David Bentley at its tip.

A confident Spurs side went at their opponents from the start and were nearly rewarded after 17 minutes. The Canaries had the left-hand upright to thank after Defoe had wriggled free of Damien Francis' challenge and unleashed a low 25-yard drive.

A weak finish from Kanoute failed to crown some neat approach play before Safri was forced to clear off the line from Defoe after captain Adam Drury's weak 24th-minute header.

The returning Gary Doherty tested Paul Robinson with a headed chance in a brief period of respite for the visitors.

It wasn't long until the one-way traffic resumed, however, Jamie Redknapp steering wide from eight yards as Green quickly closed on him.

Adam Drury beats Fredi Kanoute in the air

Norwich were virtual spectators as the North Londoners forced their Chertsey-born 'keeper into one save after another.

A fierce 25-yard effort from Defoe looked certain to break the deadlock in the 58th minute until the intervention of a strong glove.

Despite their dominance, Tottenham could easily have fallen behind on two occasions. Darren Huckerby weaved his way past several defenders before forcing Robinson to parry, and later looked a certain scorer as he rounded the 'keeper. Fortunately for Santini's side, Ledley King was alert enough to get back and make a match-saving tackle.

In between times, Green kept out Thimothee Atouba's rising drive. On this evidence it was easy to see why Sven-Goran Eriksson had called the custodian into recent England squads.

Referee Howard Webb's whistle brought to an end what had been a thoroughly entertaining 0-0 draw between two committed teams. The Canaries went home the happier, though Spurs could also take positives from the number of clear-cut chances they created.

"Robert Green showed what he can do with some great saves. He has got all the potential to go right to the very top."

Nigel Worthington

Season Review 04-05

Gary Doherty and Mark Delaney compete for a header

Saturday, September 18, 2004 Type: **Premiership** Venue: **Carrow Road** Attendance: 23,805 Referee: B Knight

Norwich City 0-0 Aston Villa

PREMIERSHIP FIXTURE HISTORY

	Pl: 4	Draws: 2	Wins ⚽	🟨	🟥
Norwich City	1	3	2	0	
Aston Villa	1	3	1	0	

STARTING LINE-UPS

🟨 McVeigh, McKenzie, Jonson, Ward, Helveg

🟣 Davis, Angel, Postma, L Moore, Whittingham

Norwich remained without a Premiership victory to their name after drawing 0-0 for the second time in a week.

Nigel Worthington kept faith with both the starting XI and midfield diamond formation that had served his team so well at Tottenham, while opposite number David O'Leary reverted to a traditional 4-4-2 shape.

The game flowed from end to end from the outset. Nolberto Solano saw a shot deflected away for a corner before Gary Holt fired over from Darren Huckerby's pass. Darius Vassell and Carlton Cole were both wasteful for Villa, while David Bentley almost embarrassed Thomas Sorensen with a clever chip.

Chances continued to come thick and fast, with the best of them falling to Cole. The on-loan Chelsea striker found himself in behind the home defence, only to be denied by a smothering save from the sprightly Robert Green. The 'keeper also did well to beat away a fierce Thomas Hitzlsperger drive in a highly entertaining opening period.

Events continued in the same vein after the break, with Huckerby keeping the Villa defence on their toes. The former Coventry City forward made several meandering runs, the first of which ended with a superbly timed tackle by Mark Delaney.

Adam Drury holds off Nolberto Solano

STATISTICS

Season	Fixture			Fixture	Season
27	3	Shots On Target		9	41
33	11	Shots Off Target		9	37
1	0	Hit Woodwork		0	2
28	3	Caught Offside		3	13
27	1	Corners		6	45
77	8	Fouls		12	92
47%	56%	Possession		44%	49%

EVENT LINE

38		**Safri (Foul)**
	HALF TIME 0 - 0	
57		Cole (Off) Angel (On)
57		Solano (Off) Davis (On)
63		Delaney (Foul)
77		**Safri (Off) McVeigh (On)**
78		Hitzlsperger (Off) Whittingham (On)
80		**Bentley (Off) McKenzie (On)**
89		**Doherty (Off) Jonson (On)**
	FULL TIME 0 - 0	

LEAGUE STANDINGS

Position (pos before)	W	D	L	F	A	Pts
19 (17) Norwich C	0	4	2	5	9	4
7 (7) Aston Villa	2	3	1	7	6	9

Though the Canaries were more than matching their opponents in most areas, it was noticeable how the visitors rarely wasted an opportunity to make Green earn his money. This was in stark contrast to the home side, whose efforts were wayward more often than not.

A 74th-minute Gary Doherty shot finally warmed the palms of Sorensen as Worthington's men sensed a chance of victory.

Referee Barry Knight then waved away a Huckerby penalty appeal before Norwich were almost punished for becoming too cavalier.

Gavin McCann missed by inches with a header, and then young debutant Steven Davis forced Green into a spectacular reflex stop.

In the end, a draw was probably a fair result. Though Villa registered three times as many shots on target as their East Anglian opponents, the Premiership newcomers enjoyed a greater share of possession.

"We are enjoying what we are doing. If we keep playing how we are playing, the results will come."

Nigel Worthington

Season Review 04-05

Marc Edworthy makes a vital sliding challenge

Saturday, September 25, 2004 Type: **Premiership** Venue: **Anfield** Attendance: **43,152** Referee: **A Wiley**

Liverpool 3-0 Norwich City

PREMIERSHIP FIXTURE HISTORY

	Pl: **4**	Draws: **0**	Wins ⚽	🟨	🟥
Liverpool	3	11	2	0	
Norwich City	1	2	6	0	

STARTING LINE-UPS

Dudek

Finnan   Carragher   Hyypia (c)   Riise

Garcia   Hamann   Alonso   Warnock

Baros   Cisse

Huckerby   Doherty

Holt   McVeigh   Francis

Safri

Drury (c)   Charlton   Fleming   Edworthy

Green

Diao, Traore, Biscan, Kirkland, Josemi

Bentley, McKenzie, Jonson, Ward, Helveg

Rafael Benitez's side turned on the style to maintain their 100% winning Premiership record at Anfield.

The three-goal deficit flattered a Norwich team that failed to score for the third consecutive League game, though there was an element of fortune about the first two strikes.

Any fears among home supporters that their Spanish manager had so far failed to implement his footballing philosophy were brushed aside in an electrifying first half-hour. The absence of the injured Steven Gerrard was barely noticeable, as Xabi Alonso raised his game with an array of crisp passes rarely seen in recent seasons.

The ball was a friend to Liverpool in the early exchanges, though Djibril Cisse didn't think so when he headed over after a mistake from Robert Green.

It was a surprise that a goal didn't arrive until the 23rd minute, Milan Baros dancing across the edge of the box from left to right before firing home a 25-yard effort that flew in off the back of Simon Charlton.

Three minutes later Luis Garcia got in on the act, capping a fine passing move with a shot from the inside-left channel that looped in off the right boot of Craig Fleming.

Gary Holt battles with Djibril Cisse

STATISTICS

Season	Fixture 🔴		🟢	Fixture	Season
44	12	Shots On Target	1		28
36	8	Shots Off Target	1		34
0	0	Hit Woodwork	0		1
16	3	Caught Offside	1		29
32	4	Corners	2		29
68	10	Fouls	12		89
55%	59%	Possession	41%		46%

EVENT LINE

23 ⚽	**Baros (Open Play)**
26 ⚽	**Garcia (Open Play)**
	HALF TIME 2 - 0
46 🔄	Doherty (Off) McKenzie (On)
46 🔄	Safri (Off) Bentley (On)
49 🟨	**Hamann (Foul)**
64 ⚽	**Cisse (Indirect Free Kick)**
65 🔄	**Alonso (Off) Diao (On)**
71 🔄	**Cisse (Off) Traore (On)**
75 🔄	McVeigh (Off) Jonson (On)
77 🔄	**Warnock (Off) Biscan (On)**
	FULL TIME 3 - 0

Nigel Worthington shuffled his pack at half-time, introducing the attack-minded Leon McKenzie and David Bentley, but it was too late.

Following further home pressure at the start of the second period, the Merseysiders extended their advantage after 64 minutes.

A centrally-positioned free-kick was touched off to Cisse some 25 yards out, and the France international unleashed a fearsome low drive beyond the despairing right hand of Green.

The remainder of the game was exhibition stuff, as Liverpool toyed with their East Anglian opponents like a cat with a mouse.

Norwich would have learned much from this footballing lesson and could take heart from the fact that they had already played some of their most demanding fixtures.

LEAGUE STANDINGS

Position (pos before)	W	D	L	F	A	Pts
7 (12) Liverpool	3	1	2	10	5	10
19 (18) Norwich C	0	4	3	5	12	4

"We've got to hand it to Liverpool, they were the better quality side on the day. But I told the lads this loss is part of a learning curve and will do us no harm."

Nigel Worthington

Season Review 04-05

Simon Charlton celebrates a rare goal

Saturday, October 2, 2004 Type: **Premiership** Venue: **Carrow Road** Attendance: **23,853** Referee: **M Messias**

Norwich City 2-2 Portsmouth

PREMIERSHIP FIXTURE HISTORY

	Pl: **1** Draws: **1**	Wins ⚽	🟨	🟥
Norwich City	0	2	1	0
Portsmouth	0	2	3	0

STARTING LINE-UPS

Green

Edworthy — Fleming — Charlton — Drury (c)

Jonson — Francis — Holt — Bentley

McKenzie — Huckerby

Kamara — Yakubu

Berger

Quashie (c) — Cisse — Faye

Taylor — Unsworth — Primus — Griffin

Hislop

McVeigh, Svensson, Ward, Helveg, Doherty

Fuller, LuaLua, Hughes, Ashdown, Mezague

Three goals in four minutes midway through the second half enlivened a game that seemed to be drifting towards a narrow away victory after Aiyegbeni Yakubu's first-half strike.

No sooner had Darren Huckerby turned home the rebound after his initial penalty had been saved than Patrik Berger restored Portsmouth's advantage, only for Simon Charlton to then pop up and make it 2-2.

The last two Division One Champions were meeting at Carrow Road in a match that could, even at this early stage of the campaign, be billed as a potential relegation six-pointer. Furthermore, Harry Redknapp was looking to avenge the first defeat he had suffered as Pompey boss.

Proceedings opened with a spate of early corners, David Bentley striking the near post with one such flag-kick.

The visitors were looking dangerous on the break, Diomansy Kamara's mesmerising run deserving a better finish.

After 37 minutes the Senegalese striker was shown how to find the net by Yakubu, the Nigeria international steering a 10-yard effort into the bottom-right corner after Robert Green had failed to hold a swerving long-range drive from Nigel Quashie.

Darren Huckerby keeps a watchful eye on the ball

EVENT LINE

37 ⚽ Yakubu (Open Play)

45 ▫ Griffin (Foul)

HALF TIME 0 - 1

60 ⇄ Kamara (Off) Fuller (On)

62 ▫ Taylor (Foul)

63 ⚽ **Huckerby (Penalty)**

65 ⚽ Berger (Indirect Free Kick)

67 ⚽ **Charlton (Corner)**

69 ▫ **Jonson (Foul)**

69 ⇄ Cisse (Off) Lua Lua (On)

72 ⇄ **Jonson (Off) McVeigh (On)**

72 ▫ Faye (Foul)

78 ⇄ Faye (Off) Hughes (On)

79 ⇄ **McKenzie (Off) Svensson (On)**

FULL TIME 2 - 2

Shaka Hislop was called upon to keep out a shot from Bentley and then to deny Damien Francis as the South Coast side went in at half-time with a one-goal advantage.

The second period offered little by way of goalmouth action, before suddenly exploding into life.

Norwich were awarded a 63rd-minute penalty after Huckerby was bundled over by Matthew Taylor, and the speedy frontman tapped home from close range after Hislop had parried his initial spot-kick.

Just two minutes later, however, all the good work was undone, Berger driving into the top-left corner from 25 yards after David Unsworth had touched a free-kick into his path.

The scoring wasn't completed, though, as Nigel Worthington's team drew level for the second time.

A 67th-minute corner found its way to Adam Drury on the left of the area, and the captain sent over a cross that Charlton glanced just inside the far post from seven yards to earn his side a valuable point.

LEAGUE STANDINGS

Position (pos before)	W	D	L	F	A	Pts
19 (19) Norwich C	0	5	3	7	14	5
13 (14) Portsmouth	2	2	3	11	11	8

PREMIERSHIP MILESTONE

Simon Charlton scored his first Premiership goal for Norwich.

"Apart from the first half at Liverpool last week, I cannot fault my players for the effort that they've put in this season."

Nigel Worthington

Season Review 04-05

Leon McKenzie tries to get the better of Thomas Gaardsoe

Saturday, October 16, 2004 Type: **Premiership** Venue: **The Hawthorns** Attendance: **26,257** Referee: **P Crossley**

West Brom 0-0 Norwich City

PREMIERSHIP FIXTURE HISTORY

	Pl: 1	Draws: 1	Wins ⚽	🟨	🟥
West Bromwich Albion	0	0	2	0	
Norwich City	0	0	2	0	

STARTING LINE-UPS

Earnshaw, Koumas, Robinson, Kuszczak, Contra

Helveg, McVeigh, Svensson, Ward, Safri

The top two Division One sides of last season played out a scoreless draw in the first ever Premiership meeting between the clubs.

Darren Huckerby was the star performer, terrorising the West Brom defence with a series of mazy runs. The pacy frontman had chosen a move to Norwich in preference to a switch to The Hawthorns during the previous campaign, and demonstrated on countless occasions why Gary Megson had tried to secure his services.

After Zoltan Gera fizzed a 20-yard effort narrowly wide, the Canaries took control.

Former Peterborough striker Leon McKenzie failed to test Russell Hoult from close range following Huckerby's ball in from the flank.

The home 'keeper then kept out Huckerby's stinging 24th-minute drive before the former Manchester City man burst through the inside-left channel, only to slice his effort towards the corner flag.

Sweden international Mattias Jonson was next to be wasteful, firing into the side-netting from close range.

At the other end, the Baggies' only genuine attempt on goal came when Robert Green was forced to turn over a miscue from team-mate Gary Holt.

Mattias Jonson climbs for a header

STATISTICS

Season	Fixture		Fixture	Season
39	2	Shots On Target	5	42
43	7	Shots Off Target	7	49
1	0	Hit Woodwork	0	2
33	1	Caught Offside	1	31
56	3	Corners	3	40
121	15	Fouls	23	125
48%	53%	Possession	47%	46%

EVENT LINE

42	🟨	**Moore (Dissent)**
		HALF TIME 0 - 0
58	⚽	**Kanu (Off) Earnshaw (On)**
59	🟨	**Johnson (Foul)**
63	🟨	McKenzie (Ung.Conduct)
69	⚽	**Greening (Off) Koumas (On)**
71	🟨	Bentley (Foul)
74	⚽	Jonson (Off) Helveg (On)
75	⚽	Bentley (Off) McVeigh (On)
80	⚽	**Gera (Off) Robinson (On)**
80	⚽	McKenzie (Off) Svensson (On)
		FULL TIME 0 - 0

LEAGUE STANDINGS

Position (pos before)	W	D	L	F	A	Pts
15 (16) West Brom	1	5	3	8	13	8
17 (20) Norwich C	0	6	3	7	14	6

> **"That was a great point for us, and two points dropped for Albion."**
> **Nigel Worthington**

The pattern of play changed little after the break, as Norwich continued to look the classier outfit.

Jonson saw a header from point-blank range repelled by Hoult on 52 minutes, while David Bentley was looking lively on the opposite wing.

The introduction of Robert Earnshaw in place of Nwankwo Kanu on 58 minutes breathed new life into West Brom.

Almost immediately, Jonathan Greening fired in a 20-yard drive that brought the best out of Green, and the shot-stopper was then alert enough to divert the ball away from the onrushing Geoff Horsfield.

Tired legs and weary bodies meant that the final half-hour wasn't a particularly edifying spectacle. Substitutes Jason Koumas and Paul McVeigh showed glimpses of skill, but there was little by way of any end product.

At the final whistle, Nigel Worthington would certainly have been the happier of the two managers. However, anyone who saw the game would tell you that with better finishing, Norwich could have been celebrating a first Premiership victory.

Season Review 04-05

Everton

Leon McKenzie forces a last-gasp challenge from Alessandro Pistone

Saturday, October 23, 2004 Type: **Premiership** Venue: **Carrow Road** Attendance: **23,871** Referee: **M Clattenburg**

Norwich City 2-3 Everton

PREMIERSHIP FIXTURE HISTORY

	Pl	Draws	Wins ⚽	🟨	🟥
	4	2			
Norwich City	1	6	2	0	
Everton	1	4	7	0	

STARTING LINE-UPS

Svensson,
Bentley,
Doherty, Ward,
Safri

Ferguson,
Watson, Yobo,
Wright,
McFadden

If Premiership football were in need of advertising, then this would have been the game to show.

Two fully committed teams served up a feast of football as the Canaries fought back bravely from a two-goal half-time deficit, only to succumb to Everton substitute Duncan Ferguson's far-post header.

The match was played at a frenetic tempo from the outset. Inside the first minute Leon McKenzie headed straight at Nigel Martyn, while Leon Osman soon forced a diving stop from Robert Green.

Then, with 10 minutes played, the visitors took the lead through Kevin Kilbane.

A quick break saw Marcus Bent feed Tim Cahill in the inside-right channel, and the former Millwall midfielder's low cross was swept home by Kilbane from eight yards out at the back post.

David Moyes' side then enjoyed a sustained spell of pressure, with Thomas Gravesen particularly influential. Home captain Adam Drury did well to prevent a second goal, but the reprieve was short-lived.

Five minutes before the break, former Ipswich forward Bent raced on to a Gravesen pass and tucked a low 15-yard effort past Green and just inside the left-hand upright.

The Norwich goalscorers share an embrace

STATISTICS

Season	Fixture			Fixture	Season
52	10	Shots On Target	9	56
61	12	Shots Off Target	4	51
2	0	Hit Woodwork	0	2
34	3	Caught Offside	1	32
51	11	Corners	4	53
134	9	Fouls	16	119
46%	49%	Possession	51%	50%

EVENT LINE

10 ⚽ Kilbane (Open Play)

37 ▯ Carsley (Foul)

40 ⚽ Bent (Open Play)

HALF TIME 0 - 2

46 ⇄ **Helveg (Off) Svensson (On)**

48 ⚽ **McKenzie (Open Play)**

57 ⚽ **Francis (Corner)**

60 ⇄ Cahill (Off) Ferguson (On)

61 ⇄ Osman (Off) Watson (On)

73 ⚽ Ferguson (Open Play)

76 ▯ Weir (Ung.Conduct)

79 ⇄ Bent (Off) Yobo (On)

83 ⇄ **Jonson (Off) Doherty (On)**

83 ⇄ **McKenzie (Off) Bentley (On)**

FULL TIME 2 - 3

With defeat staring them in the face, Nigel Worthington's team hit back shortly after the restart.

Substitute Matthias Svensson played a part in McKenzie's 48th-minute strike, releasing the former Peterborough player on the right. The forward muscled his way towards goal past Alan Stubbs and duly fired home through the legs of Martyn from six yards out at the near post.

The Canaries continued to force Everton back and deservedly drew level after 57 minutes.

A deep left-wing corner was nodded down by Mattias Jonson and Damien Francis was on hand to sweep the ball in from close range.

With the match slipping away from his high-flying team, Moyes sent on Ferguson and Steve Watson. The changes proved inspired as, following a surging run from Gravesen, Watson crossed from the right for Ferguson to power home a 73rd-minute close-range headed winner.

Lee Carsley then blocked a goalbound Francis volley as the visitors hung on for yet another away win.

LEAGUE STANDINGS

Position (pos before)	W	D	L	F	A	Pts
18 (17) Norwich C	0	6	4	9	17	6
3 (3) Everton	7	1	2	13	9	22

PREMIERSHIP MILESTONE

Leon McKenzie and Damien Francis both scored their first Premiership goals.

"We have got to be on the ball for 90 minutes, not 45."

Nigel Worthington

Season Review 04-05

Damien Francis is congratulated on his equaliser

Monday, November 1, 2004 Type: Premiership Venue: City of Manchester Stadium Attendance: 42,803 Referee: S Bennett

Manchester City 1-1 Norwich City

PREMIERSHIP FIXTURE HISTORY				
Pl: 4 Draws: 2		Wins ⚽	🟨	🟥
Manchester City	2	7	4	0
Norwich City	0	3	5	0

STARTING LINE-UPS

James

Dunne · Distin (c)

Mills · Jordan

Bosvelt · Sibierski

Flood · McManaman

Anelka · S.Wright-Phillips

McKenzie · Svensson

Huckerby · Jonson

Holt · Francis

Brennan · Edworthy

Charlton · Fleming (c)

Green

Onuoha, Fowler, Waterreus, McCarthy, B Wright-Phillips

Henderson, McVeigh, Ward, Helveg, Mulryne

Norwich recorded their seventh draw in 11 Premiership matches against a Manchester City team still searching for consistency.

The Canaries would gladly have taken a point against a rampant home side if it had been offered to them at half-time, yet they could easily have come away with all three after the second period.

Kevin Keegan's charges began brightly and went in front after just 11 minutes, Irish youngster Willo Flood marking his first Premiership start with a sweetly-struck 20-yard volley from the inside-right channel which 'keeper Robert Green should have kept out.

The Norwich custodian was given every opportunity to redeem himself, however, as the men in sky blue launched wave after wave of attacks.

Having prevented their hosts from widening the gap, Nigel Worthington's team began to create some chances of their own. Midfielder Damien Francis twice caused anxiety in the Manchester defence before netting the equaliser in the first minute of the second half.

Having just kicked off, a ball was launched into the home side's penalty area from the left. Both Danny Mills and Richard Dunne had chances to clear, but things fell kindly for Norwich following Matthias Svensson's challenge and Francis arrived on cue to level the scores from 15 yards.

Mathias Svensson rises above Danny Mills

The Canaries were in the ascendancy and David James had to earn his money on more than one occasion. With victory a distinct possibility, Norwich were perhaps guilty of pushing too many men forward – and were nearly punished.

Goalscorer Flood struck the inside of a post as Shaun Wright-Phillips led a lightning-fast break midway through the half. Then, with time nearly up, Green did brilliantly to deny Nicolas Anelka, with substitute Robbie Fowler's follow-up appearing to strike the hand of stand-in captain Craig Fleming.

Somehow the Canaries stood firm and came away with another priceless point.

A rousing finish couldn't disguise a poor second-half showing by Keegan's men, and they would have much work to do if they were to avoid becoming involved in the fight to stay in the Premiership.

"It was a very good point. We showed a lot of character, resolve and team spirit."

Nigel Worthington

Craig Fleming is challenged by Paul Dickov

Saturday, November 6, 2004 Type: **Premiership** Venue: **Carrow Road** Attendance: **23,834** Referee: **S Dunn**

Norwich City 1-1 Blackburn Rovers

PREMIERSHIP FIXTURE HISTORY

	Pl: **4**	Draws: **3**	Wins ⚽	🟨	🟥
Norwich City	1	5	3	1
Blackburn Rovers	0	4	5	1

STARTING LINE-UPS

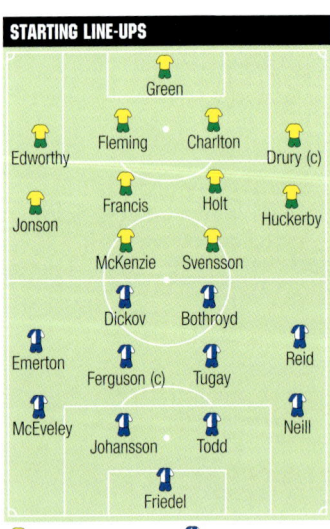

Henderson, McVeigh, Ward, Helveg, Mulryne

Flitcroft, Enckelman, Thompson, Douglas, Stead

Norwich missed a golden opportunity to record their first win in the Premiership, as they allowed 10-man Blackburn to net a late equaliser.

Mark Hughes' team saw their number reduced just before the interval when Jay Bothroyd was dismissed for violent conduct. The North-West outfit then went behind to a 56th-minute Matthias Svensson strike, but showed great character to hit back through a Paul Dickov header four minutes from time.

The Canaries made a strong start, Svensson heading against the top of the crossbar in the fifth minute. Fellow Swede Mattias Jonson then drilled an effort wide, while Leon McKenzie saw two shots blocked.

Home 'keeper Robert Green wasn't an idle spectator during the opening period, twice doing well to beat out piledrivers from Bothroyd. The Blackburn striker made a far less positive contribution to his team in the 44th minute, however, when he was sent off.

As red cards go, Bothroyd's was indisputable. Contesting possession with Jonson near the corner flag, the former Perugia frontman took exception to the Norwich player's aggressive approach and administered a firm kick to his shins.

Leon McKenzie competes with Nils-Eric Johansson

After Green successfully repelled an early second-half drive from Kerimoglu Tugay, Nigel Worthington's side made their numerical advantage count.

A free-kick eventually made its way to Svensson, stationed just beyond the left-hand upright, and the former Charlton forward drove in his first Premiership goal for the Canaries.

Being both a goal and a man up seemed to cause a crisis of confidence for the men in yellow and green. Rovers began to push forward and Craig Fleming did well to keep Dickov at bay with an excellent saving challenge.

With nine minutes remaining, Nils-Eric Johansson rattled the crossbar with a header. A goal was coming, and it duly arrived courtesy of Dickov.

Despite being one of the smallest players on the pitch, the Scot was able to meet Lucas Neill's right-wing cross following a quickly-taken free-kick with a firm downward header beyond the left hand of Green to earn his side a well-deserved point.

"The header that hit the bar was a warning. Now we have got to look forward to the next game and not dwell on this one."

Nigel Worthington

Season Review 04-05

Simon Charlton is shadowed by Radostin Kishishev

Saturday, November 13, 2004 Type: Premiership Venue: The Valley Attendance: 27,057 Referee: A Marriner

Charlton Athletic 4-0 Norwich City

PREMIERSHIP FIXTURE HISTORY

	Pl: 1 Draws: 0	Wins ⚽	🟨	🟥
Charlton Athletic	1	4	0	0
Norwich City	0	0	3	0

STARTING LINE-UPS

Kiely

Young   El Karkouri   Perry   Hreidarsson

Kishishev   Holland (c)
Murphy
Johansson   Thomas
Lisbie

McKenzie   Svensson

Huckerby
Holt   Francis   Jonson

Drury (c)
Charlton   Fleming   Edworthy

Green

🟥 Konchesky, Euell,
Jeffers, Andersen,
Fortune

🟨 Bentley, Ward,
Mulryne, Helveg
McVeigh

Norwich were given their harshest beating since returning to the Premiership, as they remained the only winless team in the top-flight.

The Canaries made a poor start to the game, finding themselves two goals down after just 21 minutes, and never fully recovered. One-time transfer target Jonatan Johansson did the early damage before substitutes Paul Konchesky and Jason Euell added gloss to the scoreline late on.

Despite being at home, Charlton boss Alan Curbishley opted to keep faith with the 4-5-1 formation that had brought success at Tottenham last time out. The policy worked, as Nigel Worthington's team struggled to combat the Addicks' attacking threat from wide areas.

The opening goal came from a free-kick in the 15th minute. Former Ipswich defender Hermann Hreidarsson climbed highest to win a header and Johansson was on hand to nod the ball into the net from close range.

The Finn, operating on the right wing, grabbed his second just six minutes later. Robert Green did well to keep out an effort from Danny Murphy, but was unable to prevent Johansson from rifling in the rebound at the back post.

David Bentley attempts to evade Danny Murphy

STATISTICS

Season	Fixture 🔴		🟡 Fixture	Season
60	11	Shots On Target	4	64
45	5	Shots Off Target	4	80
2	0	Hit Woodwork	0	3
47	7	Caught Offside	3	50
48	1	Corners	5	67
170	14	Fouls	11	181
44%	48%	Possession	52%	47%

EVENT LINE

15 ⚽ **Johansson (Indirect Free Kick)**

21 ⚽ **Johansson (Open Play)**

HALF TIME 2 - 0

46 🔄 Jonson (Off) Bentley (On)

63 🔄 Green (Off) Ward (On)

65 🔄 Holt (Off) Mulryne (On)

66 🟨 Edworthy (Foul)

74 🔄 **Lisbie (Off) Konchesky (On)**

75 ⚽ **Konchesky (Open Play)**

78 🔄 **Murphy (Off) Euell (On)**

84 🟨 Francis (Foul)

85 🔄 **Thomas (Off) Jeffers (On)**

88 ⚽ **Euell (Open Play)**

90 🟨 Bentley (Foul)

FULL TIME 4 - 0

LEAGUE STANDINGS

Position (pos before)	W	D	L	F	A	Pts
9 (11) Charlton Ath	5	3	5	17	21	18
20 (19) Norwich C	0	8	5	11	23	8

PREMIERSHIP MILESTONE

Darren Ward made his Premiership debut.

PREMIERSHIP MILESTONE

Phil Mulryne made his first Premiership appearance for Norwich.

With any game plan blown out of the water, Norwich struggled to get a foothold in the match. Gary Holt and Leon McKenzie spurned half-chances, but Charlton largely kept the visitors at arm's length.

The second period saw plenty of effort from the Carrow Road club. Darren Huckerby and former Addick Matthias Svensson posed plenty of problems for a defence that had struggled to keep clean sheets, though they couldn't conjure up an all-important goal.

With custodian Green forced off through injury, his replacement Darren Ward had little to do except twice pick the ball out of his net.

First, having just arrived from the bench, Konchesky rounded off a smart 75th-minute break down the right by sliding home from close range at the back post.

Then, a move down the opposite flank ended when Euell turned home Johansson's low cross after 88 minutes.

"The first two goals were down to bad defending, and you get taught harsh lessons in the Premiership if you make mistakes."

■ Nigel Worthington

Season Review 04-05

Darren Huckerby tries to get away from Paul Telfer

Saturday, November 20, 2004 Type: Premiership Venue: Carrow Road Attendance: 23,706 Referee: M Riley

Norwich City 2-1 Southampton

PREMIERSHIP FIXTURE HISTORY

	Pl: 4	Draws: 1		Wins 🔵	🟨	🟥
Norwich City			2	9	3	0
Southampton			1	8	6	0

STARTING LINE-UPS

Green

Fleming Charlton

Edworthy Drury (c)

Mulryne Francis

Bentley Huckerby

Svensson McKenzie

Blackstock Beattie

A Svensson Fernandes

Delap Telfer

Le Saux Dodd (c)

Kenton Lundekvam

Keller

🟡 Helveg, Ward, Safri, Jonson, Doherty

🔴 Phillips, Nilsson, Crouch, Blayney, Jakobsson

Damien Francis was the hero, as Norwich came from a goal down to record their first Premiership win of the season.

Southampton arrived at Carrow Road on the back of an important derby victory against Portsmouth and went in front through a 24th-minute James Beattie strike. The Canaries hit back, however, with a goal in each half from Francis.

The home side began brightly, Phil Mulryne forcing an early save from Kasey Keller. Referee Mike Riley then turned down a strong penalty appeal after Jason Dodd appeared to handle Darren Huckerby's cross.

Paul Telfer and Francis both worked the 'keepers before the visitors moved ahead.

There seemed little danger as Beattie prepared to strike an awkwardly bouncing ball from distance, but the former England international managed to find the back of the net with a searing effort that went in off the inside of the left-hand upright.

Far from crumbling under the weight of this hammer blow, Norwich drew level just four minutes later. Again a shot went in via a post, but this time it was Francis who steered home from 15 yards after great work by Leon McKenzie.

Damien Francis is the hero for Norwich

STATISTICS

Season	Fixture 👕		👕 Fixture	Season
72	8	Shots On Target	7	71
81	1	Shots Off Target	7	78
3	0	Hit Woodwork	0	2
54	4	Caught Offside	1	37
71	4	Corners	6	79
201	20	Fouls	14	192
47%	43%	Possession	57%	50%

EVENT LINE

24 ⚽ Beattie (Open Play)

28 ⚽ **Francis (Open Play)**

45 🟨 Kenton (Foul)

HALF TIME 1 - 1

52 ⚽ **Francis (Corner)**

60 🔁 Blackstock (Off) Phillips (On)

67 🟨 **Bentley (Foul)**

72 🔁 Telfer (Off) Nilsson (On)

83 🔁 Dodd (Off) Crouch (On)

FULL TIME 2 - 1

After a spell of further pressure from the men in yellow, Southampton had two great chances to re-establish an advantage, Dexter Blackstock seeing a swivelling shot repelled by Robert Green, with Francis then clearing off the line from Telfer.

Despite opening the second period by forcing a couple of corners of their own, the visitors went behind to a 52nd-minute flag-kick.

Craig Fleming rose well to win the initial header and Francis nodded the ball past a helpless Keller from inside the six-yard box.

David Bentley continued to trouble the Saints' defence, sending in an inviting cross from the right that evaded everyone.

From then on all the attacking came from the South Coast team, as Nigel Worthington's charges defended deeper and deeper.

A nail-biting finish ensued, but Norwich held on to secure a win that drew them level on points with their opponents.

LEAGUE STANDINGS

Position (pos before)	W	D	L	F	A	Pts
18 (20) Norwich C	1	8	5	13	24	11
17 (17) Southampton	2	5	7	13	19	11

"This was a great result today. We had to do the nasty business first, then go on and win it."

Nigel Worthington

Mark Edworthy looks to clear the danger

Saturday, November 27, 2004 Type: Premiership Venue: St Andrew's Stadium Attendance: 29,120 Referee: G Poll

Birmingham City 1-1 Norwich City

PREMIERSHIP FIXTURE HISTORY

	Pl: 1	Draws: 1	Wins 😊	🟨	🟥
Birmingham City	0	1	2	0	
Norwich City	0	1	1	0	

STARTING LINE-UPS

Taylor (Maik)

Cunningham (c) Upson

Melchiot Clapham

Savage Anderton

Johnson Dunn

Heskey Morrison

Huckerby Svensson

Brennan Bentley

Holt Mulryne

Drury (c) Edworthy

Charlton Fleming

Green

Gronkjaer,
Clemence, Yorke,
Vaesen,
Taylor (Martin)

McKenzie,
Helveg, Ward,
Doherty, Jonson

In a first meeting since the 2002 Division One play-off final, Birmingham and Norwich were again level after 90 minutes.

An early Clinton Morrison goal looked set to propel Steve Bruce's side towards only their third Premiership victory of the season, but the Canaries hit back through a 64th-minute Darren Huckerby strike.

Things began brilliantly for the West Midlands outfit, as they took the lead inside the opening 10 minutes. Summer signing Emile Heskey headed against the crossbar, with Morrison on hand to nod in the rebound from close range.

The former Crystal Palace forward had chances to complete a first-half hat-trick, but was twice thwarted by the impressive Robert Green.

Nigel Worthington's words to his players at the interval wouldn't have been kind ones, and they emerged for the second period a much stronger force. David Bentley was particularly vibrant, causing many problems with his positive running.

With 64 minutes played, Norwich got the reward their improved performance deserved.

David Bentley tries his best to win a header

STATISTICS

Season	Fixture			Fixture	Season
69	10	Shots On Target		3	75
77	6	Shots Off Target		4	85
3	1	Hit Woodwork		0	3
40	0	Caught Offside		3	57
88	6	Corners		1	72
205	14	Fouls		12	213
50%	53%	Possession		47%	47%

EVENT LINE

9	⚽	**Morrison (Open Play)**
33	🟨	**Melchiot (Dissent)**
	HALF TIME 1 - 0	
46	🔄	**Melchiot (Off) Gronkjaer (On)**
54	🔄	Brennan (Off) McKenzie (On)
58	🔄	Holt (Off) Helveg (On)
64	⚽	Huckerby (Open Play)
68	🟨	**Dunn (Foul)**
76	🔄	**Dunn (Off) Clemence (On)**
79	🔄	**Morrison (Off) Yorke (On)**
81	🟨	Bentley (Foul)
	FULL TIME 1 - 1	

LEAGUE STANDINGS

Position (pos before)	W	D	L	F	A	Pts
13 (14) Birmingham C	2	8	5	12	15	14
19 (18) Norwich C	1	9	5	14	25	12

Indecisive keeping from Maik Taylor allowed a ball from the right to reach Huckerby at the far post, and the forward slammed home from inside the six-yard box.

From this point on, only one team looked capable of winning the match. The Canaries poured forward in search of a second consecutive Premiership victory, with Matthias Svensson proving a real handful for Kenny Cunningham and Matthew Upson.

Despite their dominance, the visitors struggled to carve out anything more than half-chances in the latter stages. The best of these fell to goalscorer Huckerby, but he was unable to find a way past Taylor.

There was still time for a scare at the other end, as Robbie Savage headed weakly at Green from close range. The Welsh midfielder was furious with himself, an emotion that summed up how many of the home supporters were feeling.

Boos rang out around St Andrew's at the final whistle.

> **"When it was 1-0, I always thought we could get something from the game."**
>
> **Nigel Worthington**

Season Review 04-05

Darren Huckerby puts Sylvain Legwinski under pressure

Saturday, December 4, 2004 Type: **Premiership** Venue: **Carrow Road** Attendance: **23,755** Referee: **AG Wiley**

Norwich City 0-1 Fulham

STARTING LINE-UPS

Green

Fleming Doherty

Edworthy Drury (c)

Mulryne Helveg

Bentley Huckerby

McKenzie Svensson

Cole (c) McBride

Malbranque

Pembridge Legwinski

Diop

Bocanegra Rehman Pearce Volz

Van der Sar

Safri, Jonson, Ward, Shackell, McVeigh

Knight, Flitney, Rosenior, Radzinski, Hammond

A seventh-minute Andy Cole goal proved enough to end Norwich's recent mini-revival, as Fulham got back to winning ways.

The Nottingham-born striker rolled the ball low beyond Robert Green from 12 yards following fluent approach work involving Steed Malbranque and Brian McBride. The finish was as clinical as the move was swift, leaving the 'keeper with no chance.

Falling behind seemed to affect Nigel Worthington's men, who offered little for the home crowd to cheer in the opening 45 minutes. The Londoners were dominant in midfield, with Malbranque instigating countless dangerous attacks from his position at the head of a diamond.

Wales international Mark Pembridge twice tried his luck from long range, forcing a fine save and firing wide, while Papa Bouba Diop also stung Green's hands from distance.

The Canaries only really threatened on one occasion, Edwin van der Sar getting down well to keep out a low Mathias Svensson effort.

The second half was more evenly contested, both sides enjoying periods of dominance without finding the net.

Norwich exerted some early pressure, forcing a mistake that ultimately led to a corner.

Thomas Helveg keeps an eye on Steed Malbranque

STATISTICS

Season	Fixture		Fixture	Season
79	4	Shots On Target	9	82
91	6	Shots Off Target	6	73
3	0	Hit Woodwork	0	2
58	1	Caught Offside	3	38
77	5	Corners	4	78
225	12	Fouls	13	199
47%	49%	Possession	51%	48%

EVENT LINE

7 Cole (Open Play)

26 Volz (Foul)

HALF TIME 0 - 1

57 **Helveg (Foul)**

62 **Mulryne (Off) Safri (On)**

68 **Svensson (Off) Jonson (On)**

80 Bocanegra (Foul)

84 Cole (Dissent)

FULL TIME 0 - 1

LEAGUE STANDINGS

Position (pos before)	W	D	L	F	A	Pts
19 (19) Norwich C	1	9	6	14	26	12
14 (15) Fulham	5	2	9	18	27	17

At the other end, McBride was inches away from connecting with Cole's dangerous cross from the right.

That was as close as Fulham came to extending their advantage, though they did carve out several half-chances during the remainder of the game.

The better opportunities fell to a home side desperately in need of an equaliser.

Former Tottenham utility man Gary Doherty headed wide from a Darren Huckerby free-kick before substitute Mattias Jonson did likewise from a left-wing centre.

David Bentley fired over when he should have tested Van der Sar, and then squandered another decent opening in injury time. Again the on-loan Arsenal man drove high into the crowd, though on this occasion there was no time to try and atone for the miss.

Victory would have seen Norwich climb above the visitors in the Premiership table. As it was, defeat ensured that the gap between the two teams widened to five points.

> **"Andy Cole was in line with the defenders, there was no daylight between them, and it was a good goal."**
>
> **Nigel Worthington**

Season Review 04-05

Mattias Jonson just beats Bruno N'Gotty to the ball

Saturday, December 11, 2004 Type: **Premiership** Venue: **Carrow Road** Attendance: **23,549** Referee: B Knight

Norwich City 3-2 Bolton Wanderers

PREMIERSHIP FIXTURE HISTORY				
Pl: **1** Draws: **0**	Wins 🔵	🟨	🟥	
Norwich City	**1**	**3**	**1**	**0**
Bolton Wanderers	**0**	**2**	**3**	**0**

STARTING LINE-UPS

Green

Edworthy   Fleming (c)   Doherty   Charlton

Bentley   Helveg   Safri

Jonson   Huckerby

Svensson

Davies

Pedersen   Stelios

Speed   Campo   Okocha (c)

N'Gotty   Jaidi   Hierro   Hunt

Jaaskelainen

McVeigh, Ward,
Drury, Shackell,
Jarvis

Nolan,
Ferdinand,
Cesar, Oakes,
Ben Haim

After slipping up against Fulham in their previous match, Norwich City got their season back on track with a battling win against Bolton.

Norwich threatened in the sixth minute, Darren Huckerby collecting 'keeper Robert Green's clearance and racing down the left before laying the ball inside to Youssef Safri, whose shot flew wide.

Mattias Jonson fed Huckerby on the left five minutes later, but his low cross was cut out before it reached Mathias Svensson.

Norwich won the first corner of the game on the quarter-hour mark after Radhi Jaidi blocked Jonson's right-wing cross, but nothing came of it.

Referee Barry Knight awarded Bolton a 19th-minute penalty after Gary Doherty handled Gary Speed's long throw.

Jay-Jay Okocha stepped up and confidently slotted into the opposite corner, Green diving to his right.

Norwich equalised within a minute, Svensson heading David Bentley's right-wing cross inside the near post from eight yards.

Fernando Hierro restored Bolton's lead four minutes later, heading Stelios Giannakopoulos' left-wing corner past Green at the near post.

Mathias Svensson celebrates netting the winner

The Norwich 'keeper kept things close on 37 minutes, making an excellent save to deny Jaidi's header.

Bentley went close three minutes later, his inswinging free-kick from the left eluding everyone in the six-yard box before curling inches wide of the far post.

Norwich enjoyed most of the possession in the opening 10 minutes of the second period, though Green had to be alert to tip over a shot from Stelios.

Bruno N'Gotty and Ivan Campo were booked for late tackles on Jonson and Huckerby respectively as Norwich continued to do most of the attacking.

The Canaries won a penalty of their own on 69 minutes after Bentley was tripped by Speed.

Huckerby took it, sending Jussi Jaaskelainen the wrong way with a right-foot shot inside the 'keeper's left-hand post for 2-2.

Not surprisingly, the visitors then went on the offensive and Norwich lost some of their momentum.

Paul McVeigh fired a long-range shot over before Norwich grabbed the winner with six minutes to play, Bentley's cross from the right wing finding Svensson, whose powerful header beat the 'keeper at the far post.

"We deserved the three points. The commitment was there, and the passing was much better than last week."

Nigel Worthington

Season Review 04-05

Thomas Helveg attempts to force Mateja Kezman off the ball

Saturday, December 18, 2004 Type: Premiership Venue: Stamford Bridge Attendance: **42,071** Referee: **M Dean**

Chelsea 4-0 Norwich City

PREMIERSHIP FIXTURE HISTORY

	Pl: **4**	Draws: **0**	Wins ⚽	🟨	🟥
Chelsea	2		9	0	0
Norwich City	2		5	1	0

STARTING LINE-UPS

Cech

Ferreira   Gallas   Terry (c)   Bridge

Tiago   Makelele   Lampard

Duff   Robben

Gudjohnsen

Svensson

Huckerby   Jonson

Safri   Bentley

Helveg

Charlton   Doherty   Fleming (c)   Edworthy

Green

Drogba, Parker, Kezman, Cudicini, Johnson

McKenzie, McVeigh, Ward, Drury, Shackell

Chelsea demolished Norwich City 4-0 at Stamford Bridge, the Blues' sixth four-goal rout in their last nine Premiership matches.

The win saw the hosts move six points clear at the top of the table.

Norwich failed to record a single effort on target, their only attempt an ambitious 26th-minute chip by David Bentley which sailed over Petr Cech's bar.

Chelsea opened the scoring on 10 minutes, Damien Duff intercepting a misplaced Thomas Helveg crossfield ball in centre midfield before racing to the edge of the Norwich area and unleashing a left-foot drive into the bottom-right corner which gave 'keeper Robert Green no chance.

The Blues doubled their lead on 34 minutes, Arjen Robben collecting a poor Gary Doherty clearance and feeding Frank Lampard, who lashed the ball home with a trademark right-footer into the top-right corner from 25 yards.

Chelsea sealed the win with a third strike just before the break.

This time it was a goal entirely of their own making, with Robben the starter and sublime finisher of a wonderful move.

Quick, precise passing saw the ball move from Robben, to Lampard, to Tiago and finally back to Robben on the edge of the area, the mercurial winger blasting home with his left foot.

Youssef Safri is fouled by Tiago

STATISTICS

Season	Fixture			Fixture	Season
139	7	Shots On Target	0	84
120	4	Shots Off Target	1	97
7	0	Hit Woodwork	0	3
58	1	Caught Offside	0	59
139	7	Corners	3	84
223	13	Fouls	10	245
56%	58%	Possession	42%	47%

EVENT LINE

8   Svensson (Off) McKenzie (On)
10   **Duff (Open Play)**
34   **Lampard (Open Play)**
44   **Robben (Open Play)**

HALF TIME 3 - 0

60   **Gudjohnsen (Off) Drogba (On)**
70   Safri (Off) McVeigh (On)
76   **Tiago (Off) Parker (On)**
78   **Robben (Off) Kezman (On)**
83   **Drogba (Corner)**

FULL TIME 4 - 0

Chelsea played much better as a team in the second half, but could only manage one more goal.

Tiago went close four minutes in, his drive from the edge of the area flying inches over.

Lampard was next to threaten for the Blues, his volley from Duff's corner also going over.

Chelsea boss José Mourinho rang the first of his changes on the hour mark, replacing the ineffective Eidur Gudjohnsen with Ivory Coast striker Didier Drogba.

Robben was then denied by Green at the near post before Lampard wasted a chance by firing wide.

Despite still being some way from full fitness, Drogba's play indicated he was starting to round back into form, and he grabbed Chelsea's fourth with seven minutes to play.

Duff set him up with an excellent inswinging corner, Drogba rising high to head home.

LEAGUE STANDINGS

Position (pos before)	W	D	L	F	A	Pts
1 (1) Chelsea	13	4	1	37	8	43
17 (16) Norwich C	2	9	7	17	32	15

> **"They will be there or thereabouts, but we did alright in the first half in particular."**
>
> **Nigel Worthington**

Season Review 04-05

Youssef Safri closes down Michael Carrick

Sunday, December 26, 2004 Type: **Premiership** Venue: **Carrow Road** Attendance: **24,508** Referee: **M Riley**

Norwich City 0-2 Tottenham Hotspur

STARTING LINE-UPS

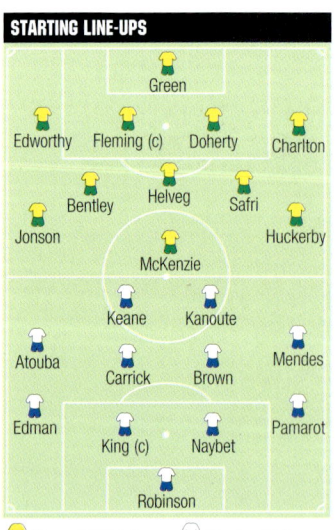

Drury, McVeigh, Mulryne, Lewis, Jarvis

Ziegler, Defoe, Redknapp, Fulop, Gardner

Norwich were punished for not turning their first-half opportunities into goals, as they went down 2-0 to Tottenham at Carrow Road.

The win made it five in a row for a rejuvenated Spurs. The Canaries were twice denied by the woodwork and saw two other efforts cleared off the line well before Spurs threatened the home goal.

If that weren't bad enough, City had three players injured in the course of the opening period.

Spurs kicked off attacking the Barclay End, Thimothee Atouba sending in a left-wing cross which eluded everyone and went out for a throw.

Norwich were forced into an early substitution after Simon Charlton limped off with a dead leg, to be replaced at left-back by Adam Drury.

Darren Huckerby then set up David Bentley, but his shot came back off a post with Paul Robinson well beaten.

The near-miss lifted the home players, Mattias Jonson's fierce drive on 14 minutes just clearing the Spurs bar before Bentley saw his shot beaten away by Robinson.

Fredi Kanoute responded for Spurs, firing over after being put through by Robbie Keane.

Jonson's lay-off opened space for Bentley on 27 minutes, but his snap-shot cleared the bar.

Gary Doherty demonstrates his aerial prowess

STATISTICS

Season	Fixture 🏆		🏆 Fixture	Season
89	5	Shots On Target	5	112
104	7	Shots Off Target	8	102
5	2	Hit Woodwork	0	5
65	6	Caught Offside	4	73
94	10	Corners	8	87
256	11	Fouls	9	232
47%	41%	Possession	59%	49%

EVENT LINE

8	🔄	**Charlton (Off) Drury (On)**
39	🔄	**Jonson (Off) McVeigh (On)**
42	🟨	**Safri (Foul)**
		HALF TIME 0 - 0
46	🔄	**Safri (Off) Mulryne (On)**
65	🔄	Atouba (Off) Ziegler (On)
71	🔄	Kanoute (Off) Defoe (On)
73	⚽	Keane (Corner)
77	⚽	Brown (Open Play)
87	🔄	Brown (Off) Redknapp (On)
		FULL TIME 0 - 2

LEAGUE STANDINGS

Position (pos before)	W	D	L	F	A	Pts
17 (17) Norwich C	2	9	8	17	34	15
7 (8) Tottenham H	8	4	7	23	18	28

PREMIERSHIP MILESTONE

24,508 The attendance of 24,508 was a Premiership record at Carrow Road.

> **"To come off the pitch with a 2-0 defeat is hard to take. We will play worse this season and win."**
>
> **Nigel Worthington**

Youssef Safri then sprained his ankle after dispossessing Kanoute inside the City six-yard box.

Jonson became the Canaries' third casualty when he left the field with a concussion minutes before the break.

Norwich went close seven minutes into the second period, Huckerby's left-wing corner finding Leon McKenzie, whose header was touched against the bar by Robinson's outstretched fingertips.

Spurs almost scored from the breakaway, Robert Green doing well to gather Keane's pass before it reached Kanoute.

Spurs broke the deadlock on 73 minutes, Pedro Mendes's right-wing corner cleared only as far as Keane, who gave Green no chance with a left-foot blast from 10 yards.

Michael Brown put a broad smile on manager Martin Jol's face four minutes later, collecting a pass from Keane before beating Green high to his left with a shot from 25 yards.

Season Review 04-05

Ryan Jarvis shows off his ball skills

Tuesday, December 28, 2004 Type: **Premiership** Venue: **Riverside Stadium** Attendance: **34,836** Referee: **H Webb**

Middlesbrough 2-0 Norwich City

PREMIERSHIP FIXTURE HISTORY

	Pl: **2** Draws: **1**	Wins ⚽	🟨	🟥
Middlesbrough	1	5	1	0
Norwich City	0	3	1	0

STARTING LINE-UPS

Schwarzer

Cooper Southgate (c)

Reiziger Queudrue

Parlour Zenden

Nemeth Downing

Hasselbaink Job

McKenzie

Huckerby Jarvis

Mulryne Helveg Bentley

Drury Doherty Fleming (c) Edworthy

Green

🟥 Morrison, Nash, McMahon, Davies, Doriva

🟡 Brennan, Crow, Gallacher, Shackell, McVeigh

Boro picked up their drive for a top-five Premiership spot with two goals in two minutes from Cameroon international Joseph-Desire Job.

Job, a replacement for injury victim Mark Viduka, took his season goal tally to five as he wrecked City's plans to swamp the Boro attack.

Norwich flooded the midfield and kept Boro at bay in the first half, but Job's quickfire strikes early in the second period sealed the points for the hosts.

Apart from Job, Boro boss Steve McLaren made one other change to his starting line-up, replacing Doriva with Szilard Nemeth.

Norwich boss Nigel Worthington made three changes to his side, inserting Adam Drury, Phil Mulryne and Ryan Jarvis.

City had the first shot on target, David Bentley forcing Mark Schwarzer into a full-length save in the second minute.

Jimmy Floyd Hasselbaink responded for Boro, but his shot from 25 yards lacked the pace to seriously trouble Robert Green.

Norwich lost Thomas Helveg in the 12th minute after he took a sickening blow to the back of the head from his own team-mate, Gary Doherty. He was replaced by Jim Brennan.

Szilard Nemeth is muscled off the ball

Green then made a superb save to deny Job, diving to push away his drive from 20 yards.

There were few real chances for the rest of the half, as both sides struggled to put together any sort of cohesive play.

Job wasted an opening five minutes into the second period, heading Stewart Downing's cross over from close range.

But he made amends two minutes later, guiding Downing's free-kick into the back of the net after the Norwich defence had left him unmarked at the far post.

Two minutes later it was game over for the Canaries, Job running on to a pass from Franck Queudrue and beating the offside trap before shooting between Green's legs.

For a time Boro threatened to run riot, but Green held the City backline together with a couple of terrific saves from Downing and Bolo Zenden.

Leon McKenzie had a chance to pull one back on 81 minutes, but Schwarzer came off his line to make the block.

"We left Job unmarked to score the first at the far post, and then we tried to play an offside trap which didn't work for the second."

Nigel Worthington

Neither man gives an inch in this battle for possession

Saturday, January 1, 2005 Type: Premiership Venue: Fratton Park Attendance: 20,015 Referee: P Dowd

Portsmouth 1-1 Norwich City

PREMIERSHIP FIXTURE HISTORY

	Pl: 1	Draws: 1	Wins ⚽	🟨	🟥
Portsmouth	0	1	3	0	
Norwich City	0	1	0	1	

STARTING LINE-UPS

Hislop

Griffin   Primus   De Zeeuw (c)   Taylor

O'Neil   Stone   Quashie   Berger

Kamara   Yakubu

McKenzie

Huckerby   Jonson

Bentley   Mulryne   Francis

Charlton   Doherty   Fleming (c)   Edworthy

Green

⚽ Faye, Fuller,
Mezague,
Ashdown,
Stefanovic

🟢 Brennan, Jarvis,
Drury, Gallacher,
Crow

Robert Green made two outstanding saves to ensure Norwich picked up a point at Fratton Park, despite playing for most of the game with 10 men.

Marc Edworthy was sent off in the fifth minute for bringing down Pompey's Diomansy Kamara as he raced for the ball following a Simon Charlton blunder.

Ten-man City were forced into defensive mode for the rest of the match, with Craig Fleming and Gary Doherty outstanding.

But ultimately it was Green who prevented Portsmouth from snatching a late victory, denying shots from Valery Mezague and full-back Andy Griffin.

Mazague was played clear by a shrewd pass from Aiyegbeni Yakubu, only to see his shot blocked by the 'keeper.

Green then dived to push away a low drive from Griffin at the foot of the post.

Norwich, who entered the game without an away win this season, took a shock lead in the ninth minute with a stunning goal by Damien Francis.

Darren Huckerby's right-wing cross was only half-cleared by Arjan De Zeeuw and Francis picked out the top-left corner with a superb right-footed volley.

Damien Francis celebrates opening the scoring

EVENT LINE

5	⬛	Edworthy (Foul)
9	⚽	Francis (Open Play)
32	🟨	**Griffin (Foul)**
35	🟨	**Yakubu (Dissent)**
43	🟨	**Taylor (Foul)**
		HALF TIME 0 - 1
61	⚽	**Yakubu (Penalty)**
61	🔁	Mulryne (Off) Brennan (On)
66	🔁	**Berger (Off) Faye (On)**
66	🔁	**Kamara (Off) Fuller (On)**
67	🔁	McKenzie (Off) Jarvis (On)
81	🔁	**Taylor (Off) Mezague (On)**
84	🔁	Huckerby (Off) Drury (On)
		FULL TIME 1 - 1

Yakubu should have equalised within a minute when Matt Taylor crossed from the left, but the Nigerian striker tucked his header into the side-netting.

Charlton then cleared Patrik Berger's shot off the line before Shaka Hislop saved at the feet of Leon McKenzie.

Kamara had the Norwich defence on the ropes again in the 16th minute, twisting his way past two defenders before shooting just wide from the edge of the penalty area.

Kamara had an early chance in the second half, firing narrowly wide with a speculative 25-yard strike. David Bentley responded by going wide for the visitors.

Pompey equalised just past the hour mark thanks to a thrice-taken penalty from Yakubu.

McKenzie was adjudged to have handled inside the box and referee Phil Dowd pointed to the spot.

Yakubu converted, but Dowd spotted Kamara encroaching and ordered a retake.

Yakubu converted again, but again Dowd ruled it out for movement by Kamara.

Once again Yakubu converted, and this time the referee let it stand.

LEAGUE STANDINGS

Position (pos before)	W	D	L	F	A	Pts
11 (10) Portsmouth	7	6	8	25	28	27
17 (18) Norwich C	2	10	9	18	37	16

"Leon McKenzie got a shove in the back, and when that happens your natural reaction is to put your arm out."

Nigel Worthington

Season Review 04-05

Thomas Helveg gets the better of John Arne Riise

Monday, January 3, 2005 Type: **Premiership** Venue: **Carrow Road** Attendance: **24,503** Referee: **H Webb**

Norwich City 1-2 Liverpool

PREMIERSHIP FIXTURE HISTORY

	Pl: 4	Draws: 1	Wins		
Norwich City	1	5	5	1
Liverpool	2	6	9	1

STARTING LINE-UPS

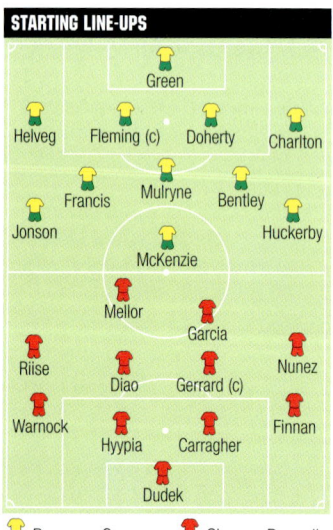

Green

Helveg Fleming (c) Doherty Charlton

Francis Mulryne Bentley

Jonson Huckerby

McKenzie

Mellor

Garcia

Riise Nunez

Diao Gerrard (c)

Warnock Finnan

Hyypia Carragher

Dudek

🟡 Brennan, Crow, Jarvis, Gallacher, Drury

🔴 Sinama-Pongolle, Hamann, Traore, Harrison, Raven

Liverpool had to work hard to complete their double over the Canaries at Carrow Road.

Not for the first time this season, City fell behind when an attacking move broke down. True to recent form, they went on to concede a second shortly afterwards.

But they battled away, Ryan Jarvis pulling one back with two minutes remaining to cause the Reds a brief scare.

Liverpool forced the first corner of the game in the fifth minute after Simon Charlton had given the ball away deep in his own half.

Norwich were reduced to 10 men for a few minutes when Mattias Jonson left the pitch to have a head wound stitched. He returned to the game with his head well bandaged.

Darren Huckerby set up a chance for Jonson, but his half-hit shot failed to trouble Reds 'keeper Jerzy Dudek.

Steven Gerrard put plenty of power into his rasping drive on 25 minutes, but it flew wide.

John Arne Riise also went wide five minutes later when well positioned inside the Norwich area.

Damien Francis was booked for a challenge on Sami Hyypia four minutes before the break, though referee Howard Webb took a more lenient view when Hyypia was flattened by Leon McKenzie a minute later.

Darren Huckerby surges past Luis Garcia

STATISTICS

Season	Fixture			Fixture	Season
99	4	Shots On Target	6		151
115	3	Shots Off Target	5		148
5	0	Hit Woodwork	0		3
70	5	Caught Offside	2		55
108	5	Corners	2		127
289	17	Fouls	20		263
46%	49%	Possession	51%		54%

EVENT LINE

41	🟨	**Francis (Foul)**
		HALF TIME 0 - 0
53	🟨	Finnan (Foul)
57	🟨	**Bentley (Foul)**
58	⚽	Garcia (Open Play)
61	🟨	Hyypia (Foul)
61	🔄	Mellor (Off) Sinama-Pongolle (On)
64	⚽	Riise (Open Play)
67	🔄	**McKenzie (Off) Crow (On)**
67	🔄	**Mulryne (Off) Brennan (On)**
77	🔄	Nunez (Off) Hamann (On)
78	🔄	**Francis (Off) Jarvis (On)**
82	🔄	Riise (Off) Traore (On)
88	⚽	**Jarvis (Open Play)**
90	🟨	Warnock (Ung.Conduct)
		FULL TIME 1 - 2

Luis Garcia had the last chance of the half in stoppage time, but he fired high into the Barclay Stand.

Norwich were first to threaten in the second period, a through-ball from Phil Mulryne just too long for McKenzie.

Huckerby's left-wing cross was then handled by Jamie Carragher, but Norwich had to settle for a corner.

With City throwing men forward Liverpool scored on the break, Riise's through-ball finding Garcia, whose first-time effort from 16 yards cleared the advancing Robert Green and settled in the back of the net.

Liverpool doubled their lead six minutes later, Florent Sinama-Pongolle's initial shot palmed away by Green and falling invitingly for Riise, who smashed home from six yards.

Jarvis came on for Francis in the 78th minute and grabbed a consolation 10 minutes later, controlling Jonson's cross on the edge of the area before beating Dudek high to his right.

LEAGUE STANDINGS

Position (pos before)	W	D	L	F	A	Pts
18 (17) Norwich C	2	10	10	19	39	16
5 (6) Liverpool	11	4	7	36	22	37

PREMIERSHIP MILESTONE
Ryan Jarvis scored his first Premiership goal.

"Up to the first goal, there was nothing in it."

Nigel Worthington

Season Review 04-05

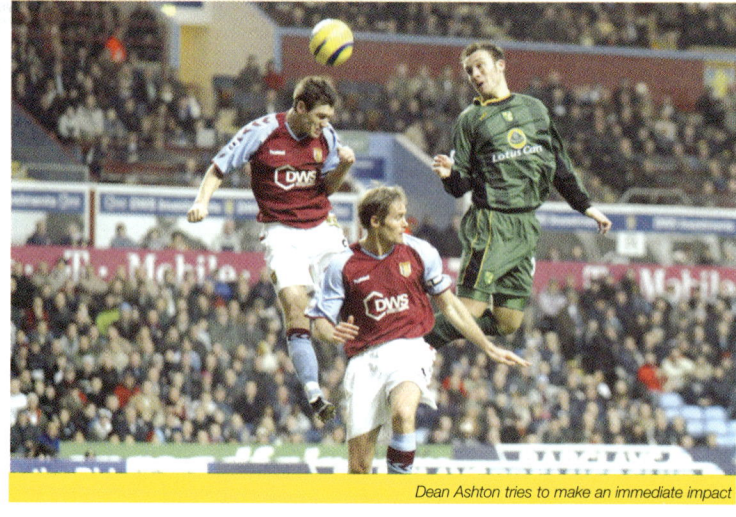

Dean Ashton tries to make an immediate impact

Saturday, January 15, 2005 Type: Premiership Venue: Villa Park Attendance: 38,172 Referee: M Riley

Aston Villa 3-0 Norwich City

PREMIERSHIP FIXTURE HISTORY

	Pl: 4	Draws: 2	Wins ⚽	🟨	🟥
Aston Villa	1	6	1	0	
Norwich City	1	4	2	0	

STARTING LINE-UPS

Sorensen

Mellberg (c)   Ridgewell

Delaney   Samuel

Hendrie   Berson

Solano   Barry

Angel   Cole

Ashton

Huckerby   Jonson

Brennan   Mulryne   Francis

Drury   Doherty   Fleming (c)   Edworthy

Green

L Moore,
Hitzlsperger,
Davis, Postma,
De la Cruz

McKenzie, Jarvis,
Crow, Gallacher,
Shackell

Aston Villa took the points after a comprehensive win over Norwich at Villa Park.

The hosts took full advantage of their struggling opposition for a change to record just their second win in nine outings.

Norwich, meanwhile, were left still searching for their first away win of the season.

The four previous games between the clubs had ended in draws, but despite some sterling work from Darren Huckerby and Mattias Jonson, the result of this one was never in doubt after two first-half goals.

Villa had an early chance, an exciting movement culminating with Juan Pablo Angel setting up Carlton Cole, only for the on-loan striker to blast his low shot wide of the upright.

Dean Ashton, Norwich's recent £3m recruit from Crewe, was showing some neat touches in his first Premiership game, though he wasted an opening when he fired wide from a good position.

Villa moved ahead on nine minutes, Liam Ridgewell heading home Nolberto Solano's free kick for his first ever senior goal for the Midlands club, the ball taking a deflection off Ashton.

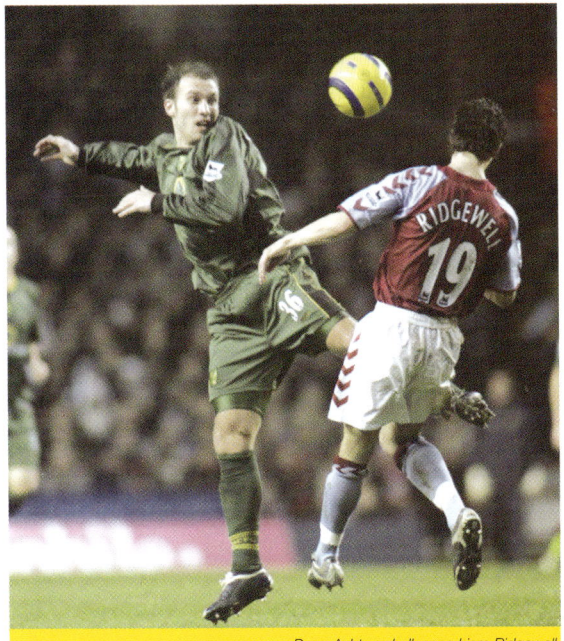

Dean Ashton challenges Liam Ridgewell

STATISTICS

Season	Fixture			Fixture	Season
122	10	Shots On Target	1	100	
121	12	Shots Off Target	6	121	
3	0	Hit Woodwork	0	5	
62	0	Caught Offside	2	72	
136	7	Corners	6	114	
342	15	Fouls	12	301	
49%	62%	Possession	38%	46%	

EVENT LINE

9 Ashton (Own Goal)

27 Hendrie (Open Play)

HALF TIME 2 - 0

46 Mulryne (Off) McKenzie (On)

74 **Cole (Off) Moore L (On)**

76 Solano (Open Play)

77 **Berson (Off) Hitzlsperger (On)**

82 **Solano (Off) Davis (On)**

85 Ashton (Off) Jarvis (On)

89 Huckerby (Off) Crow (On)

FULL TIME 3 - 0

LEAGUE STANDINGS

Position (pos before)	W	D	L	F	A	Pts
10 (10) Aston Villa	8	7	8	26	26	31
18 (18) Norwich C	2	10	11	19	42	16

PREMIERSHIP MILESTONE

Dean Ashton made his Premiership debut.

"There is still a lot to play for in the remaining 15 games, and we will keep going to the last whistle of the season."

Nigel Worthington

Angel's failure to score in the last nine games had been cited as the main reason for Villa's indifferent form of late, but there was no arguing with the Colombian's contribution on 27 minutes, setting up Lee Hendrie to convert a low shot past the advancing Robert Green.

Norwich battled away and could have pulled one back four minutes before the break if it weren't for a brilliant reflex save by Thomas Sorensen, the 'keeper flicking Ashton's shot over the bar after it had taken a deflection off Ridgewell.

Villa had two early chances in the second half, Mathieu Berson's long-distance shot flying inches wide before Green made a superb save to deny Hendrie after the midfielder had linked up with Solano on the edge of the City box.

Former Newcastle United playmaker Solano capped an outstanding performance with Villa's third goal on 76 minutes, heading home a mis-hit shot by Hendrie.

Angel went close to a late fourth for Villa, firing just over with two minutes to play.

Jim Brennan in action for Norwich

Saturday, January 22, 2005 Type: **Premiership** Venue: **Carrow Road** Attendance: **24,547** Referee: **M Messias**

Norwich City 4-4 Middlesbrough

PREMIERSHIP FIXTURE HISTORY

	Pl: 2	Draws: 2	Wins ⚽	🟨	🟥
Norwich City	0	5	0	0
Middlesbrough	0	5	3	0

STARTING LINE-UPS

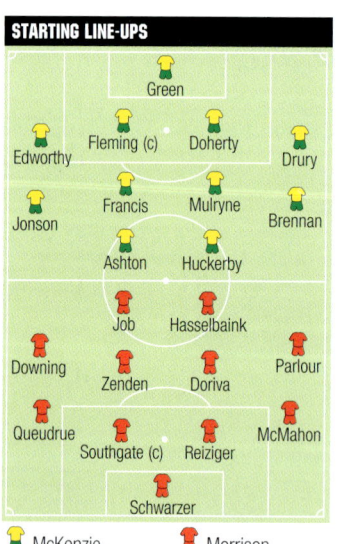

McKenzie, McVeigh, Holt, Gallacher, Jarvis

Morrison, Graham, Nash, Cooper, Nemeth

An incredible game at Carrow Road saw Norwich score three times in the last 10 minutes to salvage an unlikely 4-4 draw against Middlesbrough.

Damien Francis had given the home side an 18th-minute lead, only for braces from Jimmy Floyd Hasselbaink and Franck Queudrue to make it 4-1 after 78 minutes. Nigel Worthington's men kept going, however, and recovered through goals from Dean Ashton, Leon McKenzie and unlikely hero Adam Drury.

There was little sign of the drama that was to follow in a fairly ordinary opening period. Robert Green denied Stewart Downing and Hasselbaink pulled a left-foot effort wide, while Ashton went close with a volley at the other end.

The deadlock was broken shortly before the mid-point of the half, Francis tapping in from a yard out following Darren Huckerby's drive across the six-yard box.

Steve McClaren's team hit back in fortuitous fashion after 34 minutes, Hasselbaink diverting Downing's low shot from the left past a stranded 'keeper.

Within 10 minutes of the restart, Queudrue appeared to have put the game beyond Norwich. The visiting full-back netted twice, heading in a right-wing corner at the near post, and then side-footing home from Gareth Southgate's flick-on following a flag-kick on the opposite flank.

Damien Francis nets the first of eight goals at Carrow Road

STATISTICS

Season	Fixture			Fixture	Season
109	9	Shots On Target	15	173
129	8	Shots Off Target	7	137
5	0	Hit Woodwork	0	4
76	4	Caught Offside	2	65
119	5	Corners	8	140
313	12	Fouls	15	296
46%	45%	Possession	55%	50%

EVENT LINE

18 ⚽ **Francis (Open Play)**

22 🟨 Queudrue (Foul)

25 🟨 Parlour (Foul)

34 ⚽ Hasselbaink (Open Play)

HALF TIME 1 - 1

46 🔄 Doriva (Off) Morrison (On)

49 ⚽ Queudrue (Corner)

53 🟨 McMahon (Dissent)

55 ⚽ Queudrue (Corner)

59 🔄 **Brennan (Off) McKenzie (On)**

60 🔄 **Jonson (Off) McVeigh (On)**

64 🔄 **Mulryne (Off) Holt (On)**

74 🔄 Job (Off) Graham (On)

78 ⚽ Hasselbaink (Direct Free Kick)

80 ⚽ **Ashton (Indirect Free Kick)**

90 ⚽ **Drury (Corner)**

90 ⚽ **McKenzie (Open Play)**

FULL TIME 4 - 4

LEAGUE STANDINGS

Position (pos before)	W	D	L	F	A	Pts
19 (18) Norwich C	2	11	11	23	46	17
6 (6) Middlesbrough	10	7	7	39	33	37

PREMIERSHIP MILESTONE

Both Dean Ashton and Adam Drury netted their first Premiership goals.

PREMIERSHIP MILESTONE

24,547 The attendance of 24,547 was a Premiership record at Carrow Road.

Any lingering hopes of a Canaries comeback appeared to be snuffed out when Hasselbaink bent a 25-yard free-kick over the wall and beyond the right hand of Green 12 minutes from time. But all was not lost.

With 80 minutes played, Ashton, a transfer-window signing from Crewe, beat Mark Schwarzer to an inswinging Huckerby cross from the right to convert from close range.

Then, as the game reached the 90-minute mark, substitute McKenzie was afforded the freedom of the area to divert Huckerby's ball from the left into the bottom-right corner with his head.

It seemed that Worthington's charges would be defeated by the clock, but Drury had other ideas.

An Ashton free-kick was deflected for a corner on the left, and the full-back arrived unchallenged to nod the resulting delivery into the back of the Middlesbrough net.

> **"Even though we have only got a point, this was a moral victory."**
>
> **Nigel Worthington**

Mattias Jonson battles with Alessandro Pistone

Wednesday, February 2, 2005 Type: **Premiership** Venue: **Goodison Park** Attendance: **37,485** Referee: **A Wiley**

Everton 1-0 Norwich City

PREMIERSHIP FIXTURE HISTORY

	Pl: 4 Draws: 0	Wins ⚽	🟨	🟥
Everton	2	4	4	0
Norwich City	2	7	3	0

STARTING LINE-UPS

Martyn

Hibbert · Weir · Stubbs (c) · Pistone

Carsley · Yobo · Cahill

McFadden · Kilbane

Beattie

Huckerby · Ashton

Brennan · Holt · Francis · Jonson

Drury · Doherty · Fleming (c) · Edworthy

Green

Ferguson, Bent, Naysmith, Wright, Chadwick

Stuart, McKenzie, Gallacher, Shackell, McVeigh

A game vital to both ends of the table was settled in Everton's favour by a Gary Doherty own goal 12 minutes from time.

The Merseysiders just about deserved their victory on a pudding of a playing surface at Goodison Park. Dropped points in this fixture would have provided a resurgent Liverpool with renewed hope of stealing up on their city rivals, so the relief around the ground was tangible as the ball found its way into the back of the Norwich net.

David Moyes' men enjoyed the best of the openings during the first 45 minutes. Kevin Kilbane, a scorer at Carrow Road in October, blazed over after James Beattie had dummied a wonderful right-wing cross from James McFadden.

The young Scot was producing some of his best football since arriving at the club from Motherwell, and again delivered a dangerous centre that just evaded both Beattie and Tim Cahill.

At the other end, Darren Huckerby was the main source of danger. The sprightly forward almost beat Nigel Martyn to a weak Alessandro Pistone back-pass, and then saw strong penalty appeals turned down after clashing with David Weir.

Gary Doherty gets his head to the ball

STATISTICS

Season	Fixture	👕		👕	Fixture	Season
123	4	Shots On Target	6			115
139	14	Shots Off Target	5			134
6	0	Hit Woodwork	0			5
63	1	Caught Offside	7			83
122	3	Corners	3			122
288	12	Fouls	16			329
49%	51%	Possession	49%			46%

EVENT LINE

HALF TIME 0 - 0

46 Drury (Off) Stuart (On)

64 **Weir (Off) Ferguson (On)**

76 **Beattie (Off) Bent (On)**

78 **Doherty (Own Goal)**

81 Jonson (Off) McKenzie (On)

86 **Hibbert (Foul)**

87 **McFadden (Off) Naysmith (On)**

FULL TIME 1 - 0

LEAGUE STANDINGS

Position (pos before)		W	D	L	F	A	Pts
4 (4)	Everton	14	5	6	29	25	47
19 (19)	Norwich C	2	11	12	23	47	17

PREMIERSHIP MILESTONE

Graham Stuart made his first Premiership appearance for Norwich.

Little changed after the interval, with Everton in the ascendancy and Norwich looking dangerous on the break.

Transfer-window signing Graham Stuart was afforded a warm reception by all four sides of the ground as he came on for his Canaries debut at the start of the second period. The midfielder had played a pivotal role in keeping the Toffees in the top-flight several years earlier, and would always be welcome in the blue half of the city.

Sweden international Mattias Jonson shot weakly at Martyn, while Beattie clipped the roof of the net with a 25-yard volley, as a goal began to look increasingly likely. To that end, Duncan Ferguson was introduced in place of David Weir after 64 minutes.

Having ruffled a few feathers, the big Scot was joined in attack by Marcus Bent. Within a couple of minutes the pair had combined to help win the game, Bent forcing Robert Green into a smart parry and Doherty poking the ball into his own net under intense pressure from Ferguson.

"There's a blatant handball in the box and it's not been given."

Nigel Worthington

Season Review 04-05

Craig Fleming's looping header makes it 1-1

Saturday, February 5, 2005 Type: **Premiership** Venue: **Carrow Road** Attendance: **24,292** Referee: **C Foy**

Norwich City 3-2 West Brom

	Pl: 1	Draws: 0	Wins	⚽	🟨	🟥
Norwich City	1		3	0	0	
West Bromwich Albion	0		2	3	0	

STARTING LINE-UPS

Green
Edworthy Fleming (c) Doherty Charlton
Stuart Francis Holt
McKenzie Huckerby
Ashton
Earnshaw Campbell
Greening Gera
Wallwork Richardson
Robinson Scimeca
Clement Purse (c)
Hoult

Brennan,
McVeigh,
Gallacher,
Safri,
Jonson

Horsfield,
Kuszczak,
Gaardsoe,
Chaplow,
Kanu

Despite twice trailing, it was Norwich who triumphed in this vital battle of the bottom two at Carrow Road.

A recent improvement in form had seen West Brom draw level with their hosts on 17 points prior to kick off.

Conversely, the Canaries had picked up just two points from their last eight matches, and were in desperate need of rediscovering that winning feeling.

Nigel Worthington fielded three forwards in an attack-minded line-up, while Bryan Robson opted to start with Robert Earnshaw in preference to Geoff Horsfield as Kevin Campbell's strike partner.

The Wales international tested Robert Green after just three minutes, with Dean Ashton then calling Russell Hoult into action at the other end.

The home side continued to carve out an array of half-chances, with Darren Huckerby and Ashton guilty of several disappointing finishes. But it was the Baggies who went in front.

The normally reliable Green gifted possession to Jonathan Greening with a poor 41st-minute clearance, and the midfielder played in Earnshaw for a smart left-foot finish through the 'keeper's legs.

Gary Doherty celebrates his second-half leveller

STATISTICS

Season	Fixture			Fixture	Season
122	7	Shots On Target	8	121
140	6	Shots Off Target	7	111
5	0	Hit Woodwork	2	8
84	1	Caught Offside	1	93
125	3	Corners	3	120
346	17	Fouls	14	346
46%	45%	Possession	55%	47%

EVENT LINE

41 ⚽ Earnshaw (Open Play)

45 ⚽ **Fleming (Corner)**

45 🟨 Scimeca (Foul)

HALF TIME 1 - 1

46 🔄 **Charlton (Off) Brennan (On)**

49 ⚽ Richardson (Open Play)

62 🟨 Robinson (Foul)

62 ⚽ **Doherty (Indirect Free Kick)**

68 🔄 **Stuart (Off) McVeigh (On)**

84 🟨 Greening (Dissent)

85 ⚽ **Francis (Open Play)**

89 🔄 Greening (Off) Horsfield (On)

FULL TIME 3 - 2

LEAGUE STANDINGS

Position (pos before)	W	D	L	F	A	Pts
18 (19) Norwich C	3	11	12	26	49	20
20 (20) West Brom	2	11	13	23	49	17

PREMIERSHIP MILESTONE

Craig Fleming netted his first Premiership goal.

> **"This was a huge game, hard-fought with some good football."**
>
> **Nigel Worthington**

An interval lead seemed inevitable until captain Craig Fleming levelled matters with a looping header from Graham Stuart's right-wing corner. The effort should have been saved, but Hoult seemed more concerned with claiming a foul than with keeping the ball out.

Seemingly unfazed by the disappointment, West Brom went back in front four minutes after the restart, on-loan midfielder Kieran Richardson needing two attempts to turn Earnshaw's clipped delivery into the net.

If Fleming's header had been preventable, then Gary Doherty's certainly was. With 62 minutes on the clock, the former Tottenham man rose unchallenged to guide Huckerby's cross from the left into the bottom-right corner.

From then on the visitors looked the more likely scorers, with Green called upon to make smart saves from both Greening and Campbell.

The Canaries stole the points, however, Damien Francis rifling a 19-yard drive past the despairing right hand of Hoult from Fleming's cushioned 85th-minute knockdown.

Dean Ashton tries to make progress

Saturday, February 12, 2005 Type: Premiership Venue: Ewood Park Attendance: 20,923 Referee: S Dunn

Blackburn Rovers 3-0 Norwich City

PREMIERSHIP FIXTURE HISTORY

Pl: 4	Draws: 1		Wins 😊	🟨	🟥
Blackburn Rovers	2	12	6	0	
Norwich City	1	4	7	0	

STARTING LINE-UPS

Friedel

Todd (c) Mokoena

Nelson Johansson

Savage Tugay

Emerton Pedersen

Gallagher Dickov

Huckerby Ashton

Brennan Stuart

Holt Francis

Drury Charlton

Doherty Fleming (c)

Green

Neill, Thompson, Reid, Enckelman, Johnson

McKenzie, Safri, Gallacher, Shackell, McVeigh

A convincing 3-0 win for Blackburn saw them move eight points clear of both Norwich and the relegation zone.

Home boss Mark Hughes had taken offence to pre-match comments attributed to his opposite number Nigel Worthington that claimed his side employed bully-boy tactics. The Lancashire team did their talking on the pitch, however, with two goals from Paul Dickov and one from Morten Gamst Pedersen securing a comfortable victory.

It was the visitors who made the brighter start, Darren Huckerby squandering a great chance when he lashed the ball high over the bar from no more than eight yards out. Brad Friedel then had to be alert to keep out a drive from Damien Francis, before Rovers made the all-important breakthrough.

With 17 minutes played, Pedersen exposed both stand-in right-back Simon Charlton and 'keeper Robert Green, the Norwegian winger controlling a lofted pass from Kerimoglu Tugay and beating his marker in one movement before rifling home a 15-yard shot that went straight through the Norwich custodian.

The Canaries had a golden chance to equalise just over five minutes later when Huckerby unselfishly squared for Jim Brennan. But the former Nottingham Forest man seemed shocked by what had occurred and proceeded to miss his kick.

Kerimoglu Tugay is denied room in which to operate

STATISTICS

Season	Fixture			Fixture	Season
142	13	Shots On Target		6	128
160	5	Shots Off Target		3	143
6	0	Hit Woodwork		0	5
102	3	Caught Offside		3	87
160	12	Corners		3	128
422	11	Fouls		14	360
49%	63%	Possession		37%	45%

EVENT LINE

17	⚽ **Pedersen (Open Play)**
36	🟨 **Tugay (Foul)**
39	⚽ **Dickov (Corner)**
	HALF TIME 2 - 0
46	🔄 **Mokoena (Off) Neill (On)**
46	🔄 Brennan (Off) McKenzie (On)
62	⚽ **Dickov (Open Play)**
66	🟨 **Neill (Foul)**
70	🔄 **Emerton (Off) Reid (On)**
72	🟨 Francis (Ung.Conduct)
76	🔄 **Savage (Off) Thompson (On)**
76	🔄 Charlton (Off) Safri (On)
	FULL TIME 3 - 0

It was to prove a costly error, as Dickov struck six minutes before the break.

The diminutive Scot had earned his side a late point at Carrow Road in November, and he added another headed goal to his collection by flicking in Pedersen's near-post right-wing corner from the acutest of angles.

Robbie Savage sent a free-kick over the bar as the second half began in atrocious conditions. The hail and driving rain had receded by the time Dickov added a 62nd-minute third, the striker firing in a low 20-yard drive that Green would again have been disappointed not to save.

The 'keeper did at least prevent a late fourth, producing a marvellous double-save to deny Steven Reid and then Paul Gallagher before captain Andy Todd charged forward and crashed a 25-yard shot just past the right-hand upright.

LEAGUE STANDINGS

Position (pos before)	W	D	L	F	A	Pts
16 (16) Blackburn R	6	10	11	24	36	28
18 (18) Norwich C	3	11	13	26	52	20

> **"I have no complaints about the defeat, or the way in which Blackburn went about things."**
>
> **Nigel Worthington**

Leon McKenzie gets to grips with his marker

Monday, February 28, 2005 Type: **Premiership** Venue: **Carrow Road** Attendance: **24,302** Referee: **R Styles**

Norwich City 2-3 Manchester City

PREMIERSHIP FIXTURE HISTORY

	Pl: 4	Draws: 2	Wins ⚽	🟨	🟥
Norwich City	1	6	6	1
Manchester City	1	6	4	0

STARTING LINE-UPS

Green

Edworthy
Fleming (c) Shackell
Drury

Stuart
Francis Holt
Jonson

McKenzie Ashton

Fowler
Sibierski

Musampa
Barton Bosvelt
S Wright-Phillips

Jordan
Distin (c) Dunne
Mills

James

🟨 Safri, Gallacher,
Charlton,
McVeigh,
Henderson

🔵 Sommeil,
Weaver,
Flood,
McManaman,
B Wright-Phillips

Norwich surrendered a priceless two-goal lead, eventually succumbing to a last-gasp 3-2 defeat at the hands of Manchester City.

Strikers Dean Ashton and Leon McKenzie set the Canaries on the way to what seemed a vital victory, only for Antoine Sibierski and Robbie Fowler – with his 150th Premiership goal – to draw things level prior to the interval.

The second-half dismissal of Mattias Jonson didn't help the home side's cause, and Fowler then popped up with a cruel injury-time winner.

Kiki Musampa fired narrowly wide with the first chance of the match before Ashton netted an exquisite 12th-minute goal.

There seemed little danger as Adam Drury floated the ball forward from deep, but the former Crewe man deftly lobbed over David James and into the far-right corner of the net with the outside of his foot.

Four minutes later Carrow Road erupted again as McKenzie scored. The former Peterborough man raced clear from halfway, eventually scuffing a 15-yard shot through the legs of Sylvain Distin and beyond the committed goalkeeper.

It was all-action stuff, as Sibierski fired over and Shaun Wright-Phillips forced a save from Robert Green.

Dean Ashton challenges Danny Mills

STATISTICS

Season	Fixture			Fixture	Season
131	3	Shots On Target	6	151
145	2	Shots Off Target	9	142
5	0	Hit Woodwork	0	2
89	2	Caught Offside	0	79
131	3	Corners	12	176
373	13	Fouls	8	353
45%	39%	Possession	61%	49%

EVENT LINE

12 ⚽ **Ashton (Open Play)**
16 ⚽ **McKenzie (Open Play)**
17 🟨 **Stuart (Foul)**
25 ⚽ Sibierski (Corner)
37 ⚽ Fowler (Open Play)
HALF TIME 2 - 2
51 🟨 Barton (Foul)
66 🟥 **Jonson (2nd Bookable Offence)**
74 🔄 **Stuart (Off) Safri (On)**
76 🟨 Jordan (Foul)
90 ⚽ Fowler (Open Play)
FULL TIME 2 - 3

LEAGUE STANDINGS

Position (pos before)	W	D	L	F	A	Pts
19 (19) Norwich C	3	11	14	28	55	20
10 (12) Man City	9	9	10	34	31	36

PREMIERSHIP MILESTONE

Jason Shackell made his Premiership debut.

Then, after 25 minutes, Sibierski was left unchallenged to head home Musampa's inswinging cross from the right.

The tide turned with that goal, and City drew level eight minutes before the break.

The ball was worked to Wright-Phillips on the left, and his low centre was expertly steered home by an onrushing Fowler from around the penalty spot.

The pace of the game didn't let up after the break, though this time the currency was cards rather than goals. Joey Barton and Jonson were both cautioned for fouls before the Swede was shown a second yellow for an over-zealous 66th-minute challenge.

Nigel Worthington's men were faced with an uphill task, but seemed to have weathered the storm until Fowler netted, the striker scuffing the ball home from close range after Green had parried Wright-Phillips's low drive from the right of the six-yard box.

"We got two very good goals and we hassled and harried them, but then we stood off."
Nigel Worthington

Season Review 04-05

Darren Huckerby spins away from Joe Cole

Saturday, March 5, 2005 Type: Premiership Venue: Carrow Road Attendance: 24,506 Referee: M Halsey

Norwich City 1-3 Chelsea

PREMIERSHIP FIXTURE HISTORY

	Pl: 4	Draws: 1	Wins ⊙	⬜	🟥
Norwich City		2	7	2	0
Chelsea		1	5	7	0

STARTING LINE-UPS

🟡 McVeigh, Henderson, Ward, Charlton, Safri

🔵 Kezman, Jarosik, Cudicini, Huth, Gudjohnsen

Chelsea all but secured a second trophy of the season, winning 3-1 at Carrow Road to extend their lead at the top of the Premiership table to eight points.

José Mourinho's side dominated the first half and took a lead into the interval courtesy of Joe Cole. Spirited resistance then saw Leon McKenzie head Norwich level after 64 minutes, only for goals from substitute Mateja Kezman and Ricardo Carvalho to wrap up the victory.

Wayward shooting from Damien Duff and Frank Lampard gave the Canaries early hope, before youngster Jason Shackell had to be alert to clear an effort off his own line with a diving header.

Then, after 22 minutes of action, Cole rode a couple of challenges outside the area and fired a 20-yard drive high into the roof of Robert Green's net with his left foot.

Nigel Worthington's men responded with a couple of shots from striker Dean Ashton, while Green had to be alert to prevent Cole from reaching Lampard's diagonal pass.

The second period continued to produce plenty of goalmouth incident.

Didier Drogba was off target with a header from a free-kick, and then drove straight at the 'keeper after running on to a neat pass.

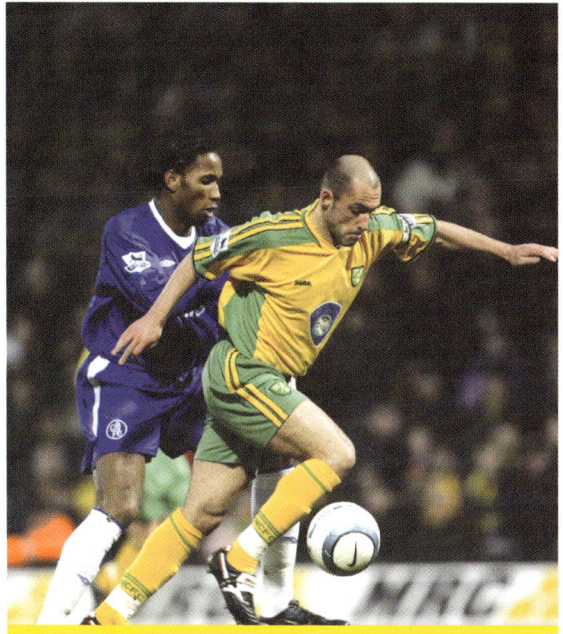
Craig Fleming is too strong for Didier Drogba

STATISTICS

Season	Fixture			Fixture	Season
136	5	Shots On Target	13		215
148	3	Shots Off Target	10		177
5	0	Hit Woodwork	0		9
91	2	Caught Offside	1		87
138	7	Corners	7		191
387	14	Fouls	15		351
45%	31%	Possession	69%		56%

EVENT LINE

19	🟨	**Drury (Foul)**
22	⚽	Cole J (Open Play)
39	🟨	Cole J (Foul)
		HALF TIME 0 - 1
58	🟨	Makelele (Foul)
64	⚽	**McKenzie (Open Play)**
67	🔄	Drogba (Off) Gudjohnsen (On)
67	🔄	Tiago (Off) Kezman (On)
71	⚽	Kezman (Open Play)
73	🔄	Duff (Off) Jarosik (On)
75	🔄	**Stuart (Off) McVeigh (On)**
79	⚽	Carvalho (Corner)
90	🔄	**McKenzie (Off) Henderson (On)**
		FULL TIME 1 - 3

A left-wing corner was glanced wide by Ashton before McKenzie became the first player in 1,025 minutes of Premiership football to beat Petr Cech, the former Peterborough man feeding the ball out to Darren Huckerby on the left and then meeting his team-mate's inswinging cross with a firm header from seven yards out.

Chelsea responded by introducing Kezman and Eidur Gudjohnsen, and were rewarded almost immediately.

The Iceland international was involved in the move that saw his fellow substitute tap his side in front from close range after Lampard had lifted the ball over a stranded 'keeper.

Eight minutes later the points were secured, Carvalho rising unchallenged to head home a left-wing corner from five yards.

The home side could take plenty of positives from their brave second-half showing, but defeat left Worthington's men with a mountain to climb if they were to stave off the threat of relegation.

LEAGUE STANDINGS

Position (pos before)	W	D	L	F	A	Pts
19 (19) Norwich C	3	11	15	29	58	20
1 (1) Chelsea	22	5	1	53	9	71

"First of all my players did well to get back into the game, but to see Kezman and Gudjohnsen warming up must have worried them a bit."

Nigel Worthington

Season Review 04-05

Gary Holt keeps tabs on Fernando Hierro

Saturday, March 19, 2005 Type: **Premiership** Venue: **Reebok Stadium** Attendance: **25,081** Referee: **P Walton**

Bolton Wanderers 1-0 Norwich City

PREMIERSHIP FIXTURE HISTORY

	Pl: 1	Draws: 0		Wins ⚽	🟨	🟥
Bolton Wanderers		1	1	3	0
Norwich City		0	0	1	0

STARTING LINE-UPS

Jaaskelainen

Hunt Ben Haim N'Gotty Candela

Nolan Hierro Speed (c)

Stelios Gardner

Davies

McKenzie Ashton

Huckerby Holt Francis Stuart

Drury Edworthy

Shackell Fleming (c)

Green

Jaidi, Poole, Campo, Okocha, Pedersen

Jonson, Doherty, Ward, Charlton, Safri

A moment of magic from Stelios Giannakopoulos was enough to beat a spirited Norwich side and lift Bolton up to fifth in the table.

European football beckoned for a team that had won seven of their last nine Premiership fixtures, while Nigel Worthington's men were now looking certainties to be plying their trade in the Championship next season.

With El-Hadji Diouf suspended, Sam Allardyce opted to push Ricardo Gardner back into the more advanced role he had begun in at Newcastle. The Canaries kept faith with the XI that had battled so bravely against Chelsea last time out.

Though Bolton shaded the first half, it was the visitors who created the two best openings.

Both chances fell to Damien Francis, the midfielder beating Jussi Jaaskelainen with a drive that flew inches wide before seeing Tal Ben Haim block another dangerous effort.

Home midfielders Gary Speed and Fernando Hierro both tried their luck from distance, while Kevin Davies felt he had been pushed over in the box.

Then, three minutes before half-time, the Trotters went in front.

Mattias Jonson closes down Stelios Giannakopoulos

STATISTICS

Season	Fixture			Fixture	Season
185	10	Shots On Target		2	138
165	6	Shots Off Target		4	152
7	1	Hit Woodwork		0	5
80	1	Caught Offside		1	92
157	7	Corners		6	144
418	20	Fouls		16	403
49%	57%	Possession		43%	45%

EVENT LINE

42	⚽	**Giannakopoulos (Corner)**
	HALF TIME 1 - 0	
56	🟨	**Hunt (Foul)**
60	🔄	Stuart (Off) Jonson (On)
73	🟨	**N'Gotty (Ung.Conduct)**
73	🟨	McKenzie (Ung.Conduct)
88	🔄	Edworthy (Off) Doherty (On)
90	🟨	**Giannakopoulos (Ung.Conduct)**
90	🔄	**Candela (Off) Jaidi (On)**
	FULL TIME 1 - 0	

LEAGUE STANDINGS

Position (pos before)	W	D	L	F	A	Pts
5 (6) Bolton W	13	7	10	38	34	46
20 (20) Norwich C	3	11	16	29	59	20

"If my lads continue to play football like that, we won't go far wrong."

Nigel Worthington

Having seen his corner from the left only half-cleared, Stelios was on hand to look up and bend a 20-yard effort high to the left of Robert Green in the Norwich goal.

Vincent Candela struck the crossbar moments later, as the game threatened to run away from the visitors.

Openings were less clear-cut after the break, with neither 'keeper being unduly troubled for much of the half.

The opportunities that did arise came late on, and all seemed to fall the way of Hierro.

Having gone close with a deflected drive seconds earlier, the Spaniard forced Green into a smart diving save to his left with another strike from distance.

With West Brom winning at Charlton earlier in the day, Worthington's men could ill afford this fourth successive defeat.

At the other end of the table, Bolton moved to within just five points of Everton, sparking thoughts of Champions League football at the Reebok Stadium next season.

Leon McKenzie appears favourite in this aerial battle

Saturday, April 2, 2005 Type: **Premiership** Venue: **Highbury** Attendance: **38,066** Referee: **A Wiley**

Arsenal 4-1 Norwich City

PREMIERSHIP FIXTURE HISTORY

	Pl: 4 Draws: 1	Wins ⚽	🟨	🟥
Arsenal		2 11	3	0
Norwich City		1 6	3	0

STARTING LINE-UPS

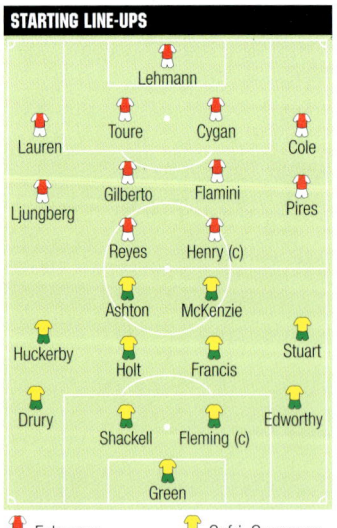

Fabregas,
Van Persie,
Clichy, Almunia,
Eboue

Safri, Svensson,
Helveg, Ward,
Doherty

Premiership top scorer Thierry Henry tore struggling Norwich apart with a hat-trick as Arsenal climbed above Manchester United in the race for England's second automatic Champions League spot.

The Gunners moved ahead on goal difference after United were held 0-0 at home by Blackburn.

Henry took his Premiership total to 25 goals with two trademark curling shots and an opportunist goal. Freddie Ljungberg added Arsenal's fourth, as the best attack in the League overwhelmed the weakest defence.

Things were looking increasingly desperate for the bottom-placed Canaries in their battle against relegation.

They now stood seven points behind the 17th-placed team with just seven games to go.

Arsenal welcomed back Brazilian midfielder Gilberto after a seven-month absence with a fractured vertebra. He replaced skipper Patrick Vieira, who was feeling the effects of France's World Cup qualifiers.

The movement of Henry and José Antonio Reyes was soon causing the Norwich defence all sorts of problems

Centre-back Craig Fleming blocked a second-minute volley from Reyes before Henry blasted a 30-yarder on the turn that was well held by 'keeper Robert Green on six minutes.

Dean Ashton puts Kolo Toure to the test

STATISTICS

Season	Fixture			Fixture	Season
245	15	Shots On Target	1		139
147	6	Shots Off Target	2		154
13	0	Hit Woodwork	0		5
74	1	Caught Offside	4		96
186	10	Corners	3		147
360	8	Fouls	11		414
56%	56%	Possession	44%		45%

EVENT LINE

19 ⚽ **Henry (Open Play)**

22 ⚽ **Henry (Open Play)**

30 ⚽ **Huckerby (Corner)**

36 🔄 **Flamini (Off) Fabregas (On)**

HALF TIME 2 - 1

50 ⚽ **Ljungberg (Open Play)**

59 🔄 Holt (Off) Safri (On)

66 ⚽ **Henry (Open Play)**

70 🔄 **Reyes (Off) van Persie (On)**

71 🔄 McKenzie (Off) Svensson (On)

73 🔄 Edworthy (Off) Helveg (On)

77 🔄 **Pires (Off) Clichy (On)**

89 🟨 **Cygan (Foul)**

FULL TIME 4 - 1

LEAGUE STANDINGS

Position (pos before)	W	D	L	F	A	Pts
2 (3) Arsenal	20	7	4	72	33	67
20 (20) Norwich C	3	11	17	30	63	20

Green came to Norwich's rescue again soon after, diving to palm away Reyes's shot after Henry had slipped the Spaniard through inside the box.

Henry made the breakthrough in the 19th minute, collecting a neat pass from Robert Pires before sidestepping two defenders and burying a low curler past Green.

The Arsenal striker added his second three minutes later, cutting into the box and beating two defenders again before bending another shot beyond Green.

Norwich responded with a goal out of nothing on the half-hour mark, Darren Huckerby cutting in from the left and sweeping a shot past Jens Lehmann after Pascal Cygan and Kolo Toure had failed to clear Green's long kick.

It was the first goal Arsenal had conceded since Peter Crouch's equaliser at Southampton on February 26.

The Gunners re-established their two-goal advantage in the 50th minute, Lauren breaking to the byline and chipping for Ljungberg to score with a close-range header.

Henry made it 4-1 on 66 minutes, reacting fastest to knock home the loose ball after Reyes had been tackled in the box.

"We stuck at it, but Arsenal's quality simply came through."

° **Nigel Worthington**

Season Review 04-05

Damien Francis gets away from Phil Neville

Saturday, April 9, 2005 Type: **Premiership** Venue: **Carrow Road** Attendance: **52,522** Referee: **H Webb**

Norwich City 2-0 Manchester United

PREMIERSHIP FIXTURE HISTORY

	Pl: **4**	Draws: **0**		Wins ⚽	🟨	🟥
Norwich City			1	3	4	0
Manchester United			3	7	4	0

STARTING LINE-UPS

Green

Fleming (c)   Shackell

Helveg   Drury

Francis   Safri

Stuart   Huckerby

Ashton   McKenzie

Saha

Fortune   Smith

Scholes   P Neville   Kleberson

Heinze   Silvestre   Ferdinand (c)   G Neville

Howard

🟩 Bentley, Svensson, Jonson, Ward, Doherty

🟥 Ronaldo, Rooney, Carroll, O'Shea, Van Nistelrooy

Goals from Dean Ashton and Leon McKenzie saw Norwich to victory over Premiership giants Manchester United at Carrow Road.

The loss was United's first in the League in 21 games.

Home 'keeper Robert Green was called into action early on, easily gathering a scuffed shot from Kleberson after good work on the right by Gary Neville.

McKenzie countered for Norwich, whipping in a dangerous cross from the left wing which was intercepted before it could reach the well-placed Damien Francis.

Cristiano Ronaldo, a 22nd-minute replacement for the injured Louis Saha, sent over a good cross from the right wing, but neither Alan Smith nor Kleberson were ready for it.

Another Ronaldo cross on the half-hour mark produced the first corner of the game, but the energetic McKenzie was on hand to head away to safety.

Norwich then forced three corners of their own, but couldn't make any of them count.

Ronaldo threatened shortly before the break, cutting in from the right before seeing his shot fly wide.

Both sides made a change at the break, Norwich midfielder David Bentley making a first appearance after a long lay-off through injury to replace Graham Stuart, while Wayne Rooney came on for Quinton Fortune.

Thomas Helveg uses all of his experience

Bentley was quickly into the action, sending a cross from the right in towards Ashton, who was unable to test Tim Howard with his header.

Good work by Darren Huckerby and Adam Drury released McKenzie, but his angled shot was saved by Howard.

Norwich wouldn't have to wait much longer for the opener, Ashton outjumping the visiting defence to head Bentley's free-kick inside the far post on 55 minutes.

Ronaldo then fired wide from the edge of the area before McKenzie doubled Norwich's advantage, blasting home a left-foot volley from 12 yards after a perfect pass from Ashton.

United created a couple of decent chances, Ruud van Nistelrooy seeing a header blocked by Craig Fleming before Green saved from Rooney.

Francis responded for Norwich, his volley blocked after Huckerby had picked him out on the edge of the United penalty area.

Rooney went close with a late chance, his ambitious shot from 35 yards tipped over by Green.

"We are still in the fight. We showed there will be a football war next week at Palace."

Nigel Worthington

Season Review 04-05

Leon McKenzie in action at Selhurst Park

Saturday, April 16, 2005 Type: **Premiership** Venue: **Selhurst Park** Attendance: **25,754** Referee: **R Styles**

Crystal Palace 3-3 Norwich City

PREMIERSHIP FIXTURE HISTORY

		Wins ⚽	🟨	🟥
Pl: **3** Draws: **1**				
Crystal Palace	0	4	2	0
Norwich City	2	6	5	0

STARTING LINE-UPS

Kiraly

Hall Sorondo

Butterfield Granville

Kolkka Leigertwood Hughes (c) Routledge

Freedman Johnson

McKenzie Ashton

Huckerby Bentley

Safri Francis

Drury Helveg

Shackell Fleming (c)

Green

Soares, Torghelle, Popovic, Speroni, Riihilahti

Holt, Svensson, Jonson, Ward, Doherty

Two teams facing the threat of an immediate return to the second tier of English football served up a six-goal thriller at Selhurst Park.

Despite propping up the table, victory at home to Manchester United in their last game meant that Norwich arrived in South London full of confidence. This was in stark contrast to Iain Dowie's side, the Eagles having lost 4-0 at Everton last time out.

The form book went out the window after just five minutes, however, as Crystal Palace took the lead, woeful marking enabling winger Joonas Kolkka to lash home Michael Hughes' floated left-wing free-kick from just wide of the six-yard box at the back post.

Ten minutes later Robert Green showed why he had been a regular member of recent England squads, diving full-length to his left to repel a 12-yard Dougie Freedman header. It was to prove a crucial stop, as the Canaries drew level midway through the half.

Midfielder Damien Francis did the hard work, bursting into the box on the left and squaring for Dean Ashton to guide the ball into an unguarded net from no more than four yards out.

Referee Rob Styles then became the focus of attention, denying the home side what appeared to be two certain penalties before half-time.

Damien Francis rises for a header

STATISTICS

Season	Fixture			Fixture	Season
152	11	Shots On Target		8	152
145	2	Shots Off Target		4	160
7	0	Hit Woodwork		0	5
77	3	Caught Offside		6	103
165	7	Corners		3	153
454	17	Fouls		21	454
47%	51%	Possession		49%	45%

EVENT LINE

5	⚽ **Kolkka (Indirect Free Kick)**
12	▯ Helveg (Ung.Conduct)
22	⚽ Ashton (Open Play)
36	▯ **Granville (Foul)**
	HALF TIME 1 - 1
46	⚽ Ashton (Open Play)
53	⚽ McKenzie (Corner)
59	▯ Shackell (Foul)
65	⇄ **Leigertwood (Off) Soares (On)**
66	▯ **Hughes (Foul)**
72	⇄ **Butterfield (Off) Torghelle (On)**
73	⚽ **Hughes (Open Play)**
83	⚽ **Johnson (Penalty)**
84	⇄ **Kolkka (Off) Popovic (On)**
88	⇄ Francis (Off) Holt (On)
88	⇄ McKenzie (Off) Svensson (On)
90	⇄ Huckerby (Off) Jonson (On)
	FULL TIME 3 - 3

First, Andy Johnson appeared to be bundled over by Jason Shackell, before Youssef Safri seemed to be guilty of handball.

Nigel Worthington's men took full advantage of these escapes, taking the lead straight from the kick off in the second period.

Fitz Hall misjudged a clip forward from the back, giving Ashton the chance to run at Gonzalo Sorondo and drive a low 15-yard effort in off the left-hand upright.

Seven minutes later the points seemed secure, as Leon McKenzie turned home Darren Huckerby's low cross from the left from inside the six-yard box.

The Eagles had other ideas, however, Hughes meeting Johnson's ball in from the right with a stunning header on the run after 73 minutes.

Then, 10 minutes later, Johnson salvaged a point from the penalty spot after Shackell was adjudged to have upended him.

LEAGUE STANDINGS

Position (pos before)	W	D	L	F	A	Pts
19 (19) Crystal Palace	6	9	18	36	57	27
20 (20) Norwich C	4	12	17	35	66	24

"The penalty was harsh, but I thought we were lucky not to give away two earlier on."

Nigel Worthington

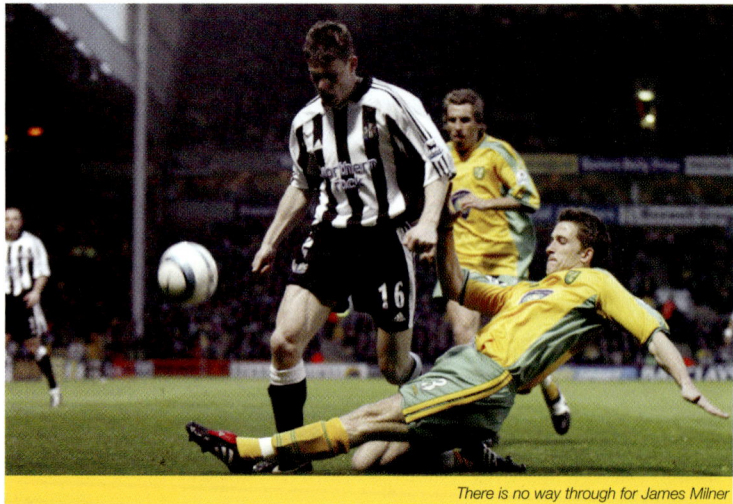

There is no way through for James Milner

Wednesday, April 20, 2005 Type: **Premiership** Venue: **Carrow Road** Attendance: **25,503** Referee: **A Marriner**

Norwich City 2-1 Newcastle United

PREMIERSHIP FIXTURE HISTORY

Pl: **3**	Draws: **0**		Wins ⚽	🟨	🟥
Norwich City		2	5	0	0
Newcastle United		1	4	0	0

STARTING LINE-UPS

Green

Helveg Fleming (c) Shackell Drury

Bentley Francis Safri Huckerby

Ashton McKenzie

Shearer (c) Ameobi

Robert N'Zogbia Butt Milner

Elliott O'Brien Boumsong Carr

Given

Jonson, Svensson, Holt, Ward, Edworthy

Ambrose, Kluivert, Harper, Ramage

Norwich continued their recent revival with a dramatic last-gasp win against a Newcastle side struggling for any kind of form.

Substitute Patrick Kluivert looked to have earned his side a point with a 90th-minute goal that cancelled out Youssef Safri's stunning effort, only for Dean Ashton to send Carrow Road into a state of delirium with a majestic headed winner.

The visitors were first to go close, captain Alan Shearer ghosting in to drive the ball just the wrong side of the left-hand upright.

Then, at the other end, striker Leon McKenzie was unable to make contact with Darren Huckerby's dangerous delivery from the left.

A dipping Laurent Robert free-kick was then spilled by Robert Green, with Shearer inexplicably failing to capitalise on the situation as he missed the target from no more than four yards out.

Robert then blazed over the bar after his initial volley had been saved before play switched to the other end, with Shay Given producing a world-class save to keep out a close-range header from Damien Francis.

Shola Ameobi drilled narrowly over the top as the game continued at a frantic pace, and there was to be no let up after the break.

Dean Ashton puts Jean-Alain Boumsong under pressure

Nigel Worthington's team came out with all guns blazing at the start of the second period, a goalmouth scramble ending with a wayward finish from Francis before Safri perfectly demonstrated how to strike a ball in the 68th minute.

Few Newcastle players would have been worried as the Morocco international lined up a shot from fully 35 yards, but his swerving strike crashed in off the woodwork to give the Canaries a priceless lead.

An Ashton goal was then ruled out for offside, with Kluivert taking full advantage to find the bottom corner of the net as the ball broke to him near the penalty spot.

A point was of little use to Norwich, and they amazingly won all three deep into injury time, former Crewe striker Ashton beating Given with a towering header from Thomas Helveg's right-wing centre, sparking scenes of great joy inside the stadium.

"I'll give him Goal of the Season."

Nigel Worthington on Youssef Safri

Dean Ashton makes a vital block

Saturday, April 23, 2005 Type: **Premiership** Venue: **Carrow Road** Attendance: **25,459** Referee: **M Atkinson**

Norwich City 1-0 Charlton Athletic

PREMIERSHIP FIXTURE HISTORY

	Pl: **1** Draws: **0**	Wins ⚽	🟨	🟥
Norwich City	1	1	1	0
Charlton Athletic	0	0	1	0

STARTING LINE-UPS

Green

Fleming (c)   Shackell

Helveg   Drury

Francis   Safri

Bentley   Jonson

Ashton   McKenzie

Jeffers

Johansson   Rommedahl

Hughes   Murphy   Holland (c)

Young   Fortune   El Karkouri   Kishishev

Kiely

🟡 Huckerby, Svensson, Holt, Ward, Brennan

🔴 Euell, Thomas, Andersen, Perry, Lisbie

Norwich's remarkable bid for Premiership survival continued apace, as Matthias Svensson netted a late winner against his former club Charlton.

Just two weeks ago the Canaries looked doomed to Championship football next season, but 10 points from the last four games had given Norwich a genuine chance of survival.

Despite some promising build-up play, chances were few and far between in the early exchanges.

Jonatan Johansson nearly found himself one-on-one with Robert Green, while a right-wing corner sailed just too high for an unmarked Dean Ashton at the other end.

As the minutes ticked by, opportunities became more prevalent.

Danny Murphy should have done better than blaze high into the crowd after Johansson's cutback from the right, while David Bentley drove just over the Charlton crossbar from 25 yards out.

Nigel Worthington's side had benefitted from the excellent link-up play between strikers Ashton and Leon McKenzie in recent weeks, and the pair combined brilliantly again on the stroke of half-time, Ashton dragging his effort just wide of the left-hand post following his partner's flick-on.

Leon McKenzie does well to keep his balance

STATISTICS

Season	Fixture		Fixture	Season
166	6	Shots On Target	6	158
174	7	Shots Off Target	5	138
5	0	Hit Woodwork	1	8
114	3	Caught Offside	0	115
166	7	Corners	8	158
474	8	Fouls	9	430
45%	56%	Possession	44%	44%

EVENT LINE

20	🟨	**Helveg (Foul)**
23	🟨	El Karkouri (Foul)
	HALF TIME 0 - 0	
62	⇄	Hughes (Off) Euell (On)
63	⇄	**Jonson (Off) Huckerby (On)**
80	⇄	**Bentley (Off) Svensson (On)**
82	⇄	Johansson (Off) Thomas (On)
88	⚽	**Svensson (Open Play)**
90	⇄	**McKenzie (Off) Holt (On)**
	FULL TIME 1 - 0	

The Addicks began the second period in the ascendancy and created several decent openings.

Talal El Karkouri forced Green into a diving stop with a drive from the edge of the box, Johansson almost got on the end of a dangerous Francis Jeffers cross, and a jinking Dennis Rommedahl run ended with a weak attempt.

Norwich responded with a long-range Damien Francis drive that was comfortably saved by Dean Kiely before McKenzie missed a gilt-edged chance.

The former Peterborough striker did well to get his head to Bentley's mis-hit volley, though he could only nod the ball wide.

With 10 minutes remaining, Svensson entered the fray. From then on, all the action seemed to revolve around the Swede, culminating in his crucial 88th-minute winner.

Having been foiled by an alert Kiely seconds after coming on to the pitch, the striker made a last-ditch challenge at the other end after Murphy had struck a post with a free-kick.

Not content with this contribution, the former Charlton man promptly won the match with an acrobatic 10-yard finish.

LEAGUE STANDINGS

Position (pos before)	W	D	L	F	A	Pts
18 (20) Norwich C	6	12	17	38	67	30
11 (10) Charlton Ath	12	9	14	40	51	45

"Winning breeds confidence, but we're still in the bottom three and can't take our feet off the pedal."

Nigel Worthington

Season Review 04-05

Kevin Phillips is off target with this effort

Saturday, April 30, 2005 **Type: Premiership** Venue: **St Mary's Stadium** Attendance: 31,944 Referee: **G Poll**

Southampton 4-3 Norwich City

PREMIERSHIP FIXTURE HISTORY				
Pl: **4** Draws: **1**	Wins	⚽	⬜	🟥
Southampton	**2**	**8**	**5**	**1**
Norwich City	**1**	**5**	**9**	**0**

STARTING LINE-UPS

Niemi

Jakobsson Higginbotham

Delap   Bernard

Redknapp Quashie

Oakley   Le Saux

Phillips (c) Crouch

Ashton McKenzie

Huckerby   Bentley

Safri Francis

Drury   Helveg

Shackell Fleming (c)

Green

🔴 Lundekvam, Telfer,   🟡 Charlton,
Camara, Smith,   Svensson, Ward,
Ormerod   Holt, Jonson

A battle of bottom-placed clubs saw Southampton edge out Norwich in a seven-goal thriller at St Mary's.

Leon McKenzie had already caused two scares when he teed up David Bentley for the visitors' third-minute opener, the striker shrugging off his marker and sending in a deep, looping cross for Bentley to steer home with a volley at the far post.

If the majority of those inside the stadium feared the worst, they were wrong. Just four minutes later, Matthew Oakley ran on to Nigel Quashie's perfectly weighted pass and drove a low effort across Robert Green and just inside the left-hand post.

Dean Ashton struck an upright and Jamie Redknapp went close with a free-kick before Harry Redknapp's men went in front midway through the half.

Rory Delap delivered an inviting centre from the right and Peter Crouch stole in to stroke home a volley from 10 yards.

The visitors moved level on 31 minutes, Danny Higginbotham sticking out a right leg to turn Darren Huckerby's low cross agonisingly beyond his helpless 'keeper.

Antti Niemi was able to keep out good efforts from both Huckerby and Bentley, with Graeme Le Saux taking advantage of these reprieves in the 39th minute.

Leon McKenzie celebrates making it 3-3 just before half-time

A free-kick from deep was nodded down by Crouch and touched back by Quashie, enabling the left-sided player to volley into the bottom-right corner from just inside the area.

That wasn't the end of the first-half scoring, however, as McKenzie grabbed a deserved goal just before the break.

The striker, who had just been penalised for a foul when hitting the woodwork, got on the end of Ashton's flick to steer the ball past the onrushing 'keeper.

The second period was no less exciting, though it lacked the drama of six goals. Norwich had the better chances, with Niemi making world-class saves to keep out Simon Charlton and McKenzie.

The stops were to prove vital, as Henri Camara emerged from the bench to crack home a low 25-yard winner in the 88th minute.

> **"I thought it was going to finish 10-10 judging by the first half, but I can't fault my players."**
> **Nigel Worthington**

Adam Drury demonstrates his commitment to the cause

Saturday, May 7, 2005 Type: **Premiership** Venue: **Carrow Road** Attendance: **25,477** Referee: **S Bennett**

Norwich City 1-0 Birmingham City

PREMIERSHIP FIXTURE HISTORY

	Pl: 1 Draws: 0		Wins ⚽	🟨	🟥
Norwich City	1	1	1		0
Birmingham City	0	0	5		1

STARTING LINE-UPS

Green

Fleming (c) Shackell

Helveg Drury

Francis Safri

Bentley Huckerby

McKenzie Ashton

Heskey Pandiani

Clapham Pennant

Nafti Johnson

Lazaridis Melchiot

Upson Cunningham (c)

Taylor (Maik)

Holt, Charlton, Svensson, Lewis, Jonson

Clemence, Morrison, Blake, Vaesen, Taylor (Martin)

Despite not being at their best, Norwich rode their luck to record a victory that saw them leap out of the relegation zone with just one game remaining.

Nigel Worthington's men were rescued by the woodwork on no fewer than three occasions, as a Dean Ashton penalty just before half-time proved enough to see off a spirited challenge from 10-man Birmingham.

The Canaries made a nervous start to proceedings, and were somewhat lucky to avoid conceding a penalty.

Former Ipswich man Jamie Clapham's shot appeared to be blocked by the arm of captain Craig Fleming, with Walter Pandiani unable to get enough power behind his follow-up strike.

The Uruguayan striker then hit the bar with his standing foot after taking a wild swing at Mario Melchiot's low delivery from the right.

With just a solitary Ashton run to show for their efforts, Norwich were handed a 31st-minute boost.

Damien Johnson inexplicably punched Denmark international Thomas Helveg in the stomach, resulting in an instantaneous red card from referee Steve Bennett.

Steve Bruce's team remained comfortable until the dying embers of the half when Darren Huckerby burst into the box and was upended by Kenny Cunningham.

Damien Francis runs with the ball

Former Crewe man Ashton took responsibility, sending Maik Taylor the wrong way from the spot.

Clinton Morrison was booked for a stupid handball that denied team-mate Emile Heskey a clear headed chance as the second period got underway, while Ashton was soon drawing a save from Taylor from an acute angle.

Leon McKenzie was denied from point-blank range as the game became more stretched, before Morrison struck the woodwork twice in quick succession.

The former Crystal Palace striker swivelled to loop a deflected 15-yard effort against the bar, and then met Jermaine Pennant's right-wing centre with a glancing header that hit almost the exact same spot.

Somehow Norwich held on to their one-goal lead, recording a victory that left them very much in charge of their own destiny.

If the Canaries could pick up a first away win of the season at Fulham, they would avoid relegation to the Championship.

"At this stage of the season, the result is more important than the performance."

Nigel Worthington

Season Review 04-05

Brian McBride opens the scoring for Fulham

Sunday, May 15, 2005 Type: **Premiership** Venue: **Craven Cottage** Attendance: **21,927** Referee: **S Dunn**

Fulham 6-0 Norwich City

PREMIERSHIP FIXTURE HISTORY

	Pl: 1 Draws: 0	Wins ⚽	🟨	🟥
Fulham	1	6	0	0
Norwich City	0	0	1	0

STARTING LINE-UPS

Van der Sar
Volz   Knight   Goma   Bocanegra
Diop
Malbranque   Boa Morte
Clark (c)
Radzinski   McBride

McKenzie   Ashton
Huckerby   Safri   Francis   Bentley
Drury   Shackell   Fleming (c)   Helveg
Green

Cole, Crossley, Pearce, Rehman, Pembridge

Holt, Jonson, Svensson, Ward, Charlton

Having battled hard to gain control of their Premiership destiny in recent weeks, Norwich exited the top-flight with something of a whimper.

The Canaries came into the game knowing that a first away win of the season would ensure survival, but suffered a six-goal drubbing that saw them return to the Championship at the first time of asking.

Nigel Worthington's men actually made an impressive start. Darren Huckerby's low drive was deflected wide, while the Fulham players had to make several last-ditch challenges.

The visitors were dealt a hammer blow after just 10 minutes, however, as Brian McBride opened the scoring.

Tomasz Radzinski created the chance, slipping a ball into the inside-right channel for his team-mate to poke under Robert Green.

Dean Ashton was then harshly penalised for a foul as he rifled in what he thought was an equaliser, before Papa Bouba Diop stunned the travelling fans by netting an exquisite 25-yard free-kick in the 35th minute.

A stretching McBride hit the bar as half-time approached, and a third goal did arrive within 10 minutes of the restart. Defender Zat Knight was the unlikely scorer, lashing a 15-yard drive through a crowd of bodies at a corner.

Youssef Safri skips away from Steed Malbranque

EVENT LINE

10 ⚽ **McBride (Open Play)**
18 🟨 Helveg (Foul)
33 🔀 Safri (Off) Holt (On)
35 ⚽ **Diop (Direct Free Kick)**
HALF TIME 2 - 0
46 🔀 Helveg (Off) Jonson (On)
54 ⚽ **Knight (Corner)**
59 🔀 Bentley (Off) Svensson (On)
72 ⚽ **Malbranque (Open Play)**
86 ⚽ **McBride (Open Play)**
87 🔀 Boa Morte (Off) Cole (On)
90 ⚽ **Cole (Open Play)**
FULL TIME 6 - 0

The Canaries, who were now completely reliant on other results going their way, went 4-0 down with 18 minutes remaining.

Luis Boa Morte was given time and space in the box, eventually picking out Steed Malbranque for a cool 12-yard finish.

As Delia Smith watched on with her fellow supporters, McBride made it five.

The American was released in the inside-left channel by Malbranque and drove the ball comfortably past Green and into the far corner.

Andy Cole, who had scored the winner in the reverse fixture, then emerged from the bench to add a cheeky sixth, the former England international deftly flicking home McBride's low cross to cap a miserable day for Norwich.

With only the result at St Mary's going in their favour, Worthington's team ended the day in 19th place.

This defeat highlighted the two main reasons for their relegation – poor away form and a leaky defence.

LEAGUE STANDINGS

Position (pos before)	W	D	L	F	A	Pts
13 (15) Fulham	12	8	18	52	60	44
19 (17) Norwich C	7	12	19	42	77	33

"The occasion got to one or two of my players, but credit must go to Fulham for a very professional performance."

Nigel Worthington

Final League Table

FINAL PREMIERSHIP TABLE – 2004-05

Pos	Name	P	Home					Away					GD	PTS
			W	D	L	F	A	W	D	L	F	A		
1	Chelsea	38	14	5	0	35	6	15	3	1	37	9	+57	95
2	Arsenal	38	13	5	1	54	19	12	3	4	33	17	+51	83
3	Man Utd	38	12	6	1	31	12	10	5	4	27	14	+32	77
4	Everton	38	12	2	5	24	15	6	5	8	21	31	-1	61
5	Liverpool	38	12	4	3	31	15	5	3	11	21	26	+11	58
6	Bolton	38	9	5	5	25	18	7	5	7	24	26	+5	58
7	Middlesbrough	38	9	6	4	29	19	5	7	7	24	27	+7	55
8	Man City	38	8	6	5	24	14	5	7	7	23	25	+8	52
9	Tottenham	38	9	5	5	36	22	5	5	9	11	19	+6	52
10	Aston Villa	38	8	6	5	26	17	4	5	10	19	35	-7	47
11	Charlton	38	8	4	7	29	29	4	6	9	13	29	-16	46
12	Birmingham	38	8	6	5	24	15	3	6	10	16	31	-6	45
13	Fulham	38	8	4	7	29	26	4	4	11	23	34	-8	44
14	Newcastle	38	7	7	5	25	25	3	7	9	22	32	-10	44
15	Blackburn	38	5	8	6	21	22	4	7	8	11	21	-11	42
16	Portsmouth	38	8	4	7	30	26	2	5	12	13	33	-16	39
17	West Brom	38	5	8	6	17	24	1	8	10	19	37	-25	34
18	Crystal Palace	38	6	5	8	21	19	1	7	11	20	43	-21	33
19	**Norwich City**	**38**	**7**	**5**	**7**	**29**	**32**	**0**	**7**	**12**	**13**	**45**	**-35**	**33**
20	Southampton	38	5	9	5	30	30	1	5	13	15	36	-21	32

First Team Appearances

Player Name	League		Carling Cup		FA Cup		Total	
	App	⚽	App	⚽	App	⚽	App	⚽
Robert Green	38	0	2	0	1	0	41	0
Adam Drury	31 (2)	1	2	0	0	0	33 (2)	1
Graham Stuart	7 (1)	0	0	0	0	0	7 (1)	0
Craig Fleming	38	1	2	0	1	0	41 (1)	1
Darren Huckerby	36 (1)	6	2	1	1	0	39 (1)	7
Philip Mulryne	8 (2)	0	0	0	0 (1)	0	8 (3)	0
Gary Holt	21 (6)	0	2	0	0	0	23 (6)	0
Mattias Jonson	19 (9)	0	1	0	1	0	21 (9)	0
David Bentley	22 (4)	2	0 (1)	0	1	0	23 (5)	2
Jim Brennan	6 (4)	0	0	0	1	0	7 (4)	0
Paul Gallacher	0	0	0	0	0	0	0	0
Leon McKenzie	24 (13)	7	0	0	0	0	24 (13)	7
Youssef Safri	13 (5)	1	1 (1)	1	0	0	14 (6)	2
Simon Charlton	22 (2)	1	1	0	1	0	24 (2)	1
Marc Edworthy	27 (1)	0	1 (1)	0	1	0	29 (2)	0
Paul McVeigh	3 (14)	1	1	0	0	0	4 (14)	1
Mathias Svensson	10 (12)	4	1 (1)	0	0	0	11 (13)	4
Damien Francis	32	7	2	0	1	0	35	7
Darren Ward	0 (1)	0	0	0	0	0	0 (1)	0
Ian Henderson	0 (3)	0	0 (1)	0	0	0	0 (4)	0
Ryan Jarvis	1 (3)	1	0	0	0 (1)	0	1 (4)	1
Jason Shackell	11	0	1	0	0	0	12	0
Thomas Helveg	16 (4)	0	1 (1)	0	1	0	18 (5)	0
Gary Doherty	17 (3)	2	2	0	1	0	20 (3)	2
Danny Crow	0 (3)	0	0	0	0 (1)	0	0 (4)	0
Dean Ashton	16	7	0	0	0	0	16	7
Own Goals	–	1	–	–	–	–	0	1

Season Review 04-05

Craig Fleming wins an important header

Saturday, January 8, 2005 Type: **FA Cup** Venue: **Upton Park** Attendance: **23,389** Referee: **U Rennie**

West Ham United 1-0 Norwich City

FA CUP FIXTURE HISTORY

Pl: **3** Draws: **1**	Wins	⚽
West Ham United	2	3
Norwich City	0	1

STARTING LINE-UPS

Walker

Repka — Ferdinand — Mackay — Powell (c)

Chadwick — Fletcher — Mullins — Noble

Rebrov

Harewood

Huckerby — Jonson

Brennan — Francis — Helveg — Bentley

Charlton — Doherty — Fleming (c) — Edworthy

Green

👕 Bywater, Cohen, McClenahan, Melville, Sofiane

👕 Gallacher, Crow, Drury, Mulryne, Jarvis

There was an upset of sorts at Upton Park, as top-six Championship side West Ham defeated Premiership strugglers Norwich.

Marlon Harewood netted the only goal of the game in the 81st minute, though it was amazing that neither side had managed to break the deadlock before then. Jimmy Walker and Robert Green were the two outstanding players on the pitch, thwarting attempts from all angles.

Alan Pardew's men were first to go close, Sergei Rebrov seeing his long-range effort acrobatically tipped over. That save was then matched at the other end, Canada international Jim Brennan being denied in similar fashion.

Chances continued to come and go, with Darren Huckerby foiled by a smothering stop. Hayden Mullins tried his luck from the edge of the box, but his venomous low strike was palmed away to safety.

An early second-half injury to David Bentley resulted in the introduction of Phil Mulryne. Within seconds of the Northern Ireland international's arrival, Huckerby had hit a post. The pacy forward ghosted behind the home defence, but watched in horror as his assured finish came back off the left-hand upright.

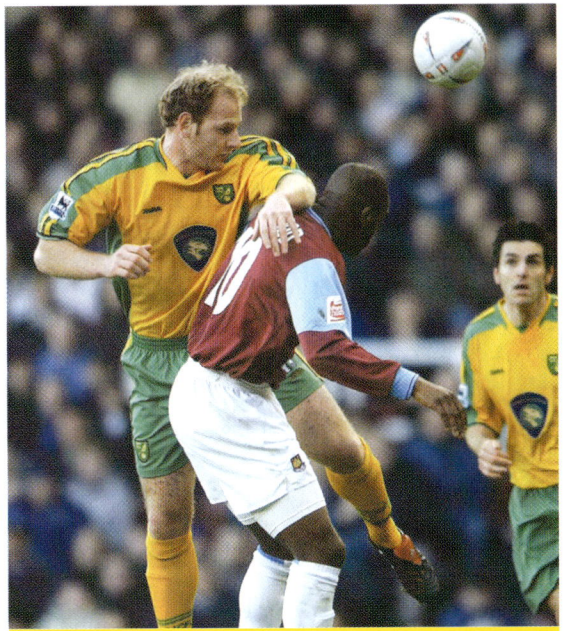
Gary Doherty makes his presence felt

STATISTICS

Fixture			Fixture
9	Shots On Target		6
6	Shots Off Target		5
0	Hit Woodwork		1
1	Caught Offside		5
10	Corners		4
11	Fouls		11

EVENT LINE

HALF TIME 0 - 0

49	⇄	Bentley (Off) Mulryne (On)
57	⇄	Helveg (Off) Jarvis (On)
81	⚽	**Harewood (Open Play)**
85	⇄	Jonson (Off) Crow (On)
90	▯	**Ferdinand (Foul)**
90	⇄	**Chadwick (Off) Cohen (On)**

FULL TIME 1 - 0

FA CUP MILESTONE

Gary Doherty, Simon Charlton and David Bentley all made their first FA Cup appearance in the colours of Norwich.

FA CUP MILESTONE

Both Craig Fleming and Darren Huckerby made their 25th FA Cup appearance.

FA CUP MILESTONE

Thomas Helveg, Mattias Jonson and Danny Crow all made their first appearance in the FA Cup.

The Canaries continued to look dangerous, and Mattias Jonson should have done better with another fantastic opportunity. Racing on to a measured pass, the Swede was unable to find a way past Walker from just eight yards out.

It wasn't all one-way traffic after the break, however, as West Ham set about claiming the scalp of their Premiership opponents.

A dangerous Rebrov free-kick made Green earn his money, though the 'keeper could no nothing to prevent Harewood's late winner.

Luke Chadwick made the goal, skipping past several challenges and then picking out his team-mate in the middle. The former Nottingham Forest striker's finish was unerring, leaving Norwich with little time in which to respond.

Nigel Worthington threw on young frontman Danny Crow in a desperate bid to force a replay, but it wasn't to be.

While the Hammers could look forward to a place in the fourth round, the visitors were now free to concentrate on their battle for top-flight survival.

> **"Today we sold ourselves short, and we sold 4,500 Norwich City supporters short."**
>
> **Nigel Worthington**

Season Review 04-05

Gary Doherty charges forward

Tuesday, September 21, 2004 Type: **Carling Cup** Venue: **Carrow Road** Attendance: **18,658** Referee: **K Friend**

Norwich City 1-0 Bristol Rovers

LEAGUE CUP FIXTURE HISTORY

Pl: 2	Draws: 1		Wins ⚽
Norwich City		1	2
Bristol Rovers		0	1

STARTING LINE-UPS

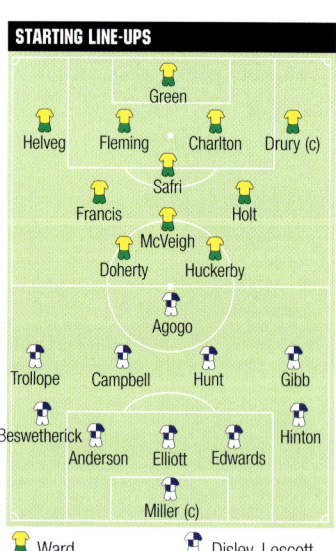

Ward, Edworthy, Jonson, Bentley, Svensson

Disley, Lescott, Forrester, Thorpe, Walker

Summer-signing Youssef Safri was the match-winner for Norwich, drilling home from distance to knock a spirited Bristol Rovers side out of the Carling Cup.

Though there was an obvious difference in the technical ability of the two sets of players, Ian Atkins' visitors played with plenty of heart and commitment. Often pinned inside their own half for lengthy spells, the Pirates defended valiantly.

Paul McVeigh was wasteful with a couple of early openings, while Gary Doherty failed to get the better of Kevin Miller in a one-on-one situation.

After Junior Agogo had seen a shot blocked during a rare foray forward, the pressure really started to mount on the League Two outfit.

A low cross from Darren Huckerby eluded everyone before Doherty headed wide from a right-wing centre. The former Tottenham man was then penalised for a foul, just as Adam Drury was turning in what he thought was the opening goal.

Robert Green wasn't completely redundant at the other end, however, keeping out efforts from both Steve Elliott and Stuart Campbell as half-time approached.

Then, with the interval just moments away, the Canaries went in front.

Junior Agogo brings the ball under control

STATISTICS

Fixture	👕	👕	Fixture
10		Shots On Target	7
6		Shots Off Target	4
0		Hit Woodwork	0
9		Caught Offside	2
5		Corners	2
14		Fouls	10

EVENT LINE

43	🟨	Anderson J (Dissent)
45	⚽	**Safri (Open Play)**
	HALF TIME 1 - 0	
59	🔄	Beswetherick (Off) Disley (On)
68	🔄	Trollope (Off) Lescott (On)
74	🔄	**Doherty (Off) Svensson (On)**
82	🔄	**McVeigh (Off) Bentley (On)**
82	🔄	Campbell (Off) Walker (On)
83	🔄	**Safri (Off) Edworthy (On)**
90	🟥	Elliott (2nd Bookable Offence)
	FULL TIME 1 - 0	

Nigel Worthington hadn't bought Safri to bolster his team's goalscoring potential, but would have been delighted at the way in which his Moroccan midfielder broke the deadlock, receiving possession some 20 yards out and arrowing a low drive just inside the far-left upright.

The timing was disastrous for Rovers and they still seemed to be in a state of shock as the second period got underway, neat interplay between Drury and Huckerby ending with the forward shooting tamely into the side-netting.

Norwich were unable to kill the game off, and visiting substitute Craig Disley would have forced extra-time had his late strike from inside the six-yard box been more accurate.

Defender Elliott was harshly dismissed in the 90th minute, the former Derby man receiving his second yellow card of the match for an innocuous trip on Huckerby.

LEAGUE CUP MILESTONE
Gary Doherty made his 10th League Cup appearance and his first in the competition for Norwich.

LEAGUE CUP MILESTONE
Youssef Safri marked his first League Cup appearance for Norwich with his first goal in the competition.

LEAGUE CUP MILESTONE
Thomas Helveg made his first League Cup appearance.

LEAGUE CUP MILESTONE
Simon Charlton, David Bentley, Darren Huckerby and Matthias Svensson all made their first League Cup appearance for Norwich.

"Bristol came here to frustrate us, but I was happy with our performance."

Nigel Worthington

Darren Huckerby scores from the penalty spot

Wednesday, October 27, 2004 Type: **Carling Cup** Venue: **St James' Park** Attendance: **42,153** Referee: **P Dowd**

Newcastle United 2-1 Norwich City

LEAGUE CUP FIXTURE HISTORY

Pl: **1** Draws: **0** Wins ⚽

Newcastle United	1	2
Norwich City	0	1

STARTING LINE-UPS

Harper

Hughes Johnsen Bramble Bernard

Milner Jenas (c) Ambrose Robert

Ameobi Kluivert

Svensson Doherty

Huckerby Jonson

Holt Francis

Drury (c) Edworthy

Shackell Fleming

Green

Given, O'Brien, Bowyer, Bellamy, Shearer

Ward, Helveg, Safri, Bentley, Henderson

Norwich crashed out of the Carling Cup at St James' Park, as they failed to recover from a poor first-half showing.

The Canaries were second-best in every department during the opening period, and went behind inside two minutes.

A Laurent Robert corner wreaked havoc inside the penalty area, with Jermaine Jenas eventually bundling the ball over the line in the ensuing scramble.

Patrick Kluivert played a part in the goal, and the Dutchman was soon involved again.

Great skill and vision from the former Barcelona striker set Shola Ameobi away, but the finish didn't match the approach play.

The same could be said of a rare opportunity at the other end, Marc Edworthy heading over from Damien Francis's pinpoint delivery.

A plethora of chances came and went for Newcastle, beginning with a curling Ameobi effort that may well have gone in had it not struck the head of Jason Shackell. Robert Green was then called upon to make a smart double-save, foiling ex-Ipswich man Darren Ambrose and then Jenas.

Mathias Svensson keeps a close eye on the ball

STATISTICS

Fixture			Fixture
16	Shots On Target		3
6	Shots Off Target		5
0	Hit Woodwork		1
0	Caught Offside		2
13	Corners		4
18	Fouls		12

EVENT LINE

2	⚽ Jenas (Corner)
42	⚽ Ameobi (Penalty)
HALF TIME 2 - 0	
46	🔄 Holt (Off) Safri (On)
56	⚽ Huckerby (Penalty)
61	🔄 Doherty (Off) Henderson (On)
65	🟨 **Ambrose (Foul)**
65	🔄 Drury (Off) Helveg (On)
69	🔄 **Robert (Off) Bellamy (On)**
77	🟨 **Bernard (Foul)**
83	🔄 **Ameobi (Off) Bowyer (On)**
87	🟨 **Bowyer (Foul)**
90	🟨 Huckerby (Foul)
FULL TIME 2 - 1	

Both Kluivert and Robert were unlucky not to score as the interval approached, before referee Phil Dowd handed the home side a penalty.

Midfielder Ambrose tumbled in the box, and Ameobi put his earlier misses aside as he converted the chance.

There was still time for Nigel Worthington's men to hit the bar before half-time, and the Magpies failed to heed the warning.

A 56th-minute push on Matthias Svensson saw another spot-kick awarded, which Darren Huckerby duly tucked away.

Having squandered a two-goal lead in their August Premiership meeting, the team in black and white became increasingly anxious. There were several moments of uncertainty, though the visitors were unable to carve out any more clear-cut chances.

With time running out Graeme Souness's charges almost made it 3-1, James Milner finding Ambrose in space, only for the youngster to direct his drive straight at Green.

LEAGUE CUP MILESTONE
Both Jason Shackell and Mattias Jonson made their first League Cup appearance.

LEAGUE CUP MILESTONE
Darren Huckerby netted his first League Cup goal for Norwich.

> **"Our 'keeper was certainly the busier, but I thought it was a good game of football."**
> **Nigel Worthington**

Player Profiles

Player Profiles

Paul **Gallacher**

Date of Birth August 16, 1979
Place of Birth Glasgow
Previous Clubs Dundee United, Airdrieonians (Loan), Gillingham (Loan), Sheffield Wednesday (Loan)
Norwich Debut N/A
Total Norwich Appearances 0
Total Norwich Clean Sheets 0
Squad No 21

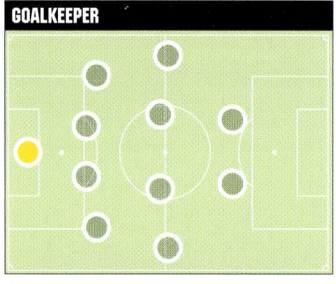

GOALKEEPER

Scotland international goalkeeper Paul Gallacher joined the Canaries in the summer of 2004.

The 25-year-old stopper was signed from Dundee United on a free transfer with his contract at Tannadice coming to an end.

Despite already being a full international, Paul was signed as a player with experience under his belt but also with great potential for the future, and his arrival provided both cover and competition for Robert Green, Darren Ward and Joe Lewis.

During his first season at Carrow Road Paul played 12 reserve games, but with first-team opportunities being limited he took in a loan spell at Coca-Cola Championship side Gillingham over the Christmas period.

His month at the Priestfield Stadium was cut short however, after Darren Ward sustained a knee injury in training and Paul was recalled to Carrow Road. Eleven games on the first-team bench followed.

A spell in Coca-Cola League One with promotion-chasing Sheffield Wednesday followed later in the season, with Paul enjoying regular first-team action during a goalkeeping crisis at Hillsborough.

STATS 2004-05

	App			
League	0	0	0	0
FA Cup	0	0	0	0
Carling Cup	0	0	0	0
Total	0	0	0	0

Robert **Green**

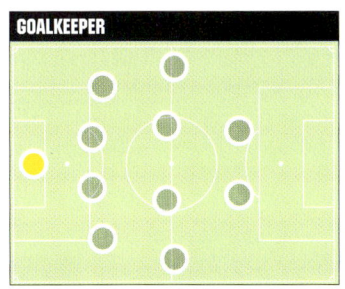

GOALKEEPER

Date of Birth January 18, 1980
Place of Birth Surrey
Previous Clubs N/A
Norwich Debut April 11, 1999 vs Ipswich Town (H) 0-0
Total Norwich Appearances 195 (1)
Total Norwich Clean Sheets 63
Squad No 1

A product of the Canaries' youth system Robert Green has progressed through the ranks at Carrow Road to become recognised as one of the best young goalkeepers in the country.

After making his Canary debut in the dramatic setting of a local East Anglian derby back in 1999, Robert had to patiently bide his time as understudy to Andy Marshall before establishing himself as City's Number One at the start of the 2001-02 season.

Robert played a starring role in City's 2003-04 First Division championship-winning campaign, and a memorable season saw him come third in the Club's Player of the Year award and also earn his first call-up to the England squad.

Promotion to the Barclays Premiership for the 2004-05 season saw Robert take his talents to the top level, where he continued to impress and establish himself as a regular in the England squad.

An agile, commanding and impressive 'keeper, Robert made his international debut during England's recent tour of the US, coming on as a half-time substitute in the 3-2 victory over Colombia in New Jersey on May 31, 2005.

Robert has all the necessary qualities to become England's Number One for years to come.

STATS 2004-05	App			
League	38	6	0	0
FA Cup	1	0	0	0
Carling Cup	2	1	0	0
Total	**41**	**7**	**0**	**0**

Player Profiles

Joe **Lewis**

Date of Birth October 6, 1987
Place of Birth Broome, Suffolk
Previous Clubs N/A
Norwich Debut N/A
Total Norwich Appearances 0
Total Norwich Clean Sheets 0
Squad No 30

Goalkeeper Joe Lewis is currently the youngest member of the Canaries' squad and the latest player to come through the Academy to earn a professional contract at Carrow Road.

Although Joe has still to make his full Canary debut, he almost took Ryan Jarvis' mantel as the Club's youngest-ever player when he made seven appearances on the first-team bench during the Club's 2003-04 championship-winning season as a 15-year-old schoolboy.

A regular at both Academy and reserve team level, Joe got a taste of first-team action at Carrow Road in August 2004 during a pre-season friendly with Real Mallorca.

Joe has represented England at various schoolboy and youth levels, and last season linked up with the national Under-18 side.

A boyhood Norwich fan and now clearly a Canary 'keeper of the future, Joe's undoubted qualities were further recognised when he was handed his first professional contract in October 2004 following his 17th birthday.

Norwich City have a great tradition of producing and fielding great goalkeepers and in Joe Lewis it certainly looks as though that trend is going to continue into the future.

GOALKEEPER

STATS 2004-05	App	🏳	🟨	🟥
League	0	0	0	0
FA Cup	0	0	0	0
Carling Cup	0	0	0	0
Total	**0**	**0**	**0**	**0**

Darren **Ward**

Date of Birth May 11, 1974
Place of Birth Worksop
Previous Clubs Mansfield Town, Notts County, Nottingham Forest
Norwich Debut November 13, 2004 vs Charlton Athletic (A) 0-4
Total Norwich Appearances 0 (1)
Total Norwich Clean Sheets 0
Squad No 12

A vastly experienced goalkeeper, 31-year-old Darren Ward joined the Canaries in July 2004 on a two-year deal from Nottingham Forest.

A full Wales international, Darren began his career with Mansfield Town before moving on to Notts County and subsequently Nottingham Forest.

An excellent shot-stopper, Darren commands his area extremely well, and with over 450 League appearances to his name is one of the most experienced members of Nigel Worthington's squad.

Opportunities in his first season at Carrow Road were limited due to the form of Robert Green, but Darren established himself as the Club's second-choice 'keeper ahead of Paul Gallacher and Joe Lewis.

He made nine reserve team appearances and was on the bench as City's substitute 'keeper on 29 occasions, tasting action just once following Robert Green's departure with injury during the second half of City's match away at Charlton.

STATS 2004-05

	App	🔲	🟨	🟥
League	0 (1)	0	0	0
FA Cup	0	0	0	0
Carling Cup	0	0	0	0
Total	**0 (1)**	**0**	**0**	**0**

Player Profiles

Jim **Brennan**

Date of Birth December 8, 1977
Place of Birth Toronto
Previous Clubs Bristol City, Huddersfield Town (Loan), Nottingham Forest
Norwich Debut November 29, 2003 vs Crewe Alexandra (H) 1-0
Total Norwich Appearances 15 (12)
Total Norwich Goals 2
Squad No 11

Canada international Jim Brennan joined the Canaries in the summer of 2003 and played 15 games during his first season at Carrow Road, as City clinched the Nationwide First Division championship title and promotion to the Barclays Premiership.

Aged 28, Jim started his career in this country with Bristol City before moving on to Nottingham Forest. It was at the City Ground that he developed the reputation as an attacking left-back with an eye for goal.

An experienced player who normally operates at left-back but also has the ability to perform in midfield, Jim's flexibility has seen him become a valuable member of the Canaries' squad.

Jim's Canary career began frustratingly, as a deep-seated abductor muscle injury delayed his debut at the start of the 2003-04 season.

A number of minor injuries last season subsequently limited him to just six starts in the 2004-05 Barclays Premiership campaign and he will be hoping to make a bigger impression on the first-team picture in 2005-06.

DEFENDER

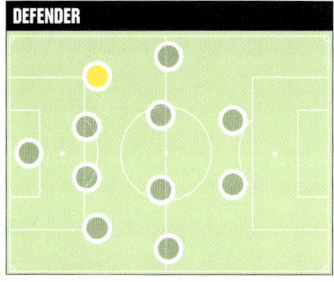

STATS 2004-05				
	App	⚽	🟨	🟥
League	6 (4)	0	0	0
FA Cup	1	0	0	0
Carling Cup	0	0	0	0
Total	7 (4)	0	0	0

Simon **Charlton**

Date of Birth October 25, 1971
Place of Birth Huddersfield
Previous Clubs Huddersfield Town, Southampton, Birmingham City, Bolton Wanderers
Norwich Debut August 14, 2004 vs Crystal Palace (H) 1-1
Total Norwich Appearances 24 (2)
Total Norwich Goals 1
Squad No 16

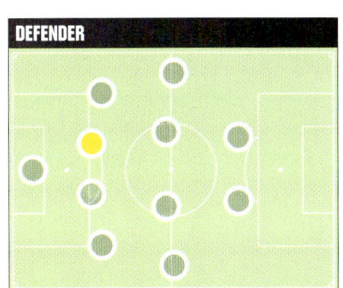

DEFENDER

Defender Simon Charlton joined the Canaries in July 2004 and immediately flew out to Malaysia to join up with his new team-mates at their pre-season training camp.

A vastly experienced defender, Simon began his career with Huddersfield Town before enjoying successful spells with Southampton, Birmingham City and Bolton Wanderers, from whom he left to join the Canaries for a fee of £250,000.

With the ability to operate at either centre-back or left-back, Simon's versatility and experience were of great benefit to the Canaries in last season's Barclays Premiership campaign. He even chipped in with his first goal in over six years during the 2-2 draw with Portsmouth at Carrow Road.

Although not a tall defender, Simon is surprisingly competitive in the air as well as on the deck, where his swift and determined tackling skills often helped the Canaries to convert defence into attack.

A popular character in the dressing room and well-respected by the supporters, Simon could well prove to be a vital cog in the Canaries' 2005-06 Coca-Cola Championship campaign.

STATS 2004-05	App	⚽	🟨	🟥
League	22 (2)	1	1	0
FA Cup	1	0	0	0
Carling Cup	1	0	0	0
Total	24 (2)	1	1	0

Player Profiles

Gary **Doherty**

Date of Birth January 31, 1980
Place of Birth Donegal
Previous Clubs Luton Town, Tottenham Hotspur
Norwich Debut August 25, 2004 vs Manchester United (A) 1-2
Total Norwich Appearances 20 (3)
Total Norwich Goals 2
Squad No 27

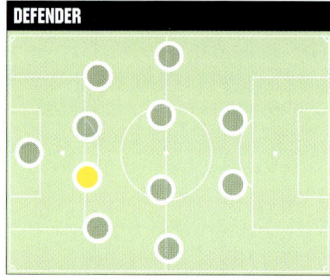

DEFENDER

STATS 2004-05				
	App	⚽	🟨	🟥
League	17 (3)	2	0	0
FA Cup	1	0	0	0
Carling Cup	2	0	0	0
Total	20 (3)	2	0	0

Republic of Ireland international defender Gary Doherty joined the Canaries from Tottenham Hotspur a week into the 2004-05 season.

The big centre-back signed a three-year deal at Carrow Road and his arrival stiffened up competition for places in the City defence.

He began his career at Luton Town and soon developed a reputation as a utility man after also playing successfully as a striker during his time at Kenilworth Road.

A big money move to Tottenham followed, but Gary was unable to cement a regular place in the starting line-up at White Hart Lane and jumped at the chance of joining the Canaries.

He started his Norwich career by playing in a forward role and found the net in only his second game for City as his equaliser earned a point from a trip to St James' Park.

His preferred position is at centre back and he partnered Craig Fleming at the heart of the Canary defence for several months during the 2004-05 season before losing his place in the side to Jason Shackell.

Always a threat at set-pieces, Gary can chip in with his fair share of goals even when operating in defence.

With both international and Premiership experience to call upon, a lot will be expected of Gary in his second season at Carrow Road.

Adam **Drury**

Date of Birth August 29, 1978
Place of Birth Cambridge
Previous Clubs Peterborough United
Norwich Debut March 31, 2001 v Grimsby Town (H) 2-1
Total Norwich Appearances 172 (2)
Total Norwich Goals 3
Squad No 3

After enjoying three-and-a-half years of outstandingly consistent form – which were backed up by the Player of the Year award in 2002-03 and lifting the Nationwide First Division Championship trophy in 2004 – the Canaries' return to the top flight of English football certainly proved to be a challenging one for Adam Drury.

Adam joined the Club from Peterborough United in March 2001 and immediately solved the Canaries' long-running left-back problems.

A quick, decisive and determined defender, Adam has improved year-on-year since arriving at Carrow Road.

After captaining the Club to promotion in 2003-04, Adam suffered a loss of form at the end of 2004 and for the first time in his Canary career was dropped from the first team. As many expected, with Adam being the model professional, he soon regained his form and returned to the team a better player.

The attacking side of Adam's game has continued to improve and it was fitting reward for his determined efforts in winning back his place that it was he who headed home City's late equaliser in the thrilling 4-4 Carrow Road match with Middlesbrough.

DEFENDER

STATS 2004-05				
	App	⚽	🟨	🟥
League	31 (2)	1	2	0
FA Cup	0	0	0	0
Carling Cup	2	0	0	0
Total	33 (2)	1	2	0

Craig **Fleming**

Date of Birth October 6, 1971
Place of Birth Halifax
Previous Clubs Halifax Town, Oldham Athletic
Norwich Debut August 9, 1997 vs Wolverhampton Wanderers (H) 0-2
Total Norwich Appearances 322 (8)
Total Norwich Goals 11
Squad No 5

DEFENDER

Club Captain Craig Fleming enjoyed an ever-present season during the Canaries' 2004-05 Barclays Premiership adventure.

After joining the Club from Oldham Athletic in the summer of 1997, Craig has been the linchpin of the Canaries' defence, and in October 2004 celebrated his 300th game for the Club.

His consistency and commitment to the Canary cause saw him voted Player of the Year at the end of the historic 2003-04 championship-winning campaign, and he carried his good form into 2004-05.

Craig started last season with Simon Charlton as his central defensive partner and then had a spell alongside Gary Doherty before young Jason Shackell broke into the team at the tail end of the season.

Craig clearly had a major impact on the development of young Jason and was always on hand with words of advice for the youngster, who made such an impression upon his elevation to the first team.

With a testimonial season on the horizon, Craig will be looking to continue his impressive Carrow Road career as his number of appearances heads towards the 400 mark.

STATS 2004-05	App	⚽	🟨	🟥
League	38	1	2	0
FA Cup	1	0	0	0
Carling Cup	2	0	0	0
Total	41	1	2	0

Matthieu **Louis-Jean**

Date of Birth February 22, 1976
Place of Birth Mont-St-Aignan
Previous Clubs Le Havre, Nottingham Forest
Norwich Debut N/A
Total Norwich Appearances 0
Total Norwich Goals 0
Squad No 2

French right-back Matthieu Louis-Jean joined the Canaries in July 2005 from Nottingham Forest in a swap deal, with Canary midfielder Gary Holt moving in the opposite direction to the City Ground.

An experienced defender, Matthieu racked up almost 200 League appearances during his six years at the City Ground and at the time of his departure was Forest's longest-serving player.

He initially joined Forest on loan from Le Havre, but soon impressed to earn himself a permanent switch across the Channel as Forest paid £500,000 for his services.

Matthieu immediately set about the task of making the Forest right-back berth his own and after becoming a consistent performer at the City Ground he became widely recognised as one of most competent attacking full-backs outside of the Premiership.

He will find a trio of familiar faces when he arrives at the Canaries' Colney Training Centre in the shape of former Forest men Jim Brennan, Darren Ward and Darren Huckerby, and his arrival at Carrow Road will increase boss Nigel Worthington's defensive options during the 2005-06 season.

DEFENDER

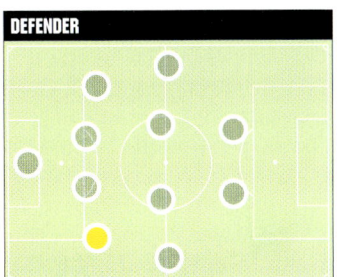

STATS 2004-05				
	App	⚽	🟨	🟥
League	22 (3)	0	5	0
FA Cup	1	0	0	0
Carling Cup	3	0	1	0
Total	26 (3)	0	6	0

Player Profiles

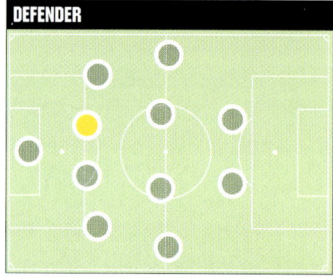

DEFENDER

Jason **Shackell**

Date of Birth September 27, 1983
Place of Birth Stevenage
Previous Clubs N/A
Norwich Debut April 5, 2003 vs Derby County (A) 1-2
Total Norwich Appearances 18 (2)
Total Norwich Goals 0
Squad No 4

Patience was certainly the key for Jason Shackell during 2004-05 as the young defender broke into the first team and produced a number of Man of the Match displays during the final weeks of the season.

A product of the Canaries' Youth Academy, Jason has always impressed at youth and reserve team level and now looks certain to make a place at the heart of the City defence his own for many years to come.

A powerful and extremely competitive defender, Jason is confident on the ball and his height can cause problems for opposing defences at set-pieces.

However, defending is very much Jason's art and his timing, whether in aerial challenges or on the deck, is excellent, often enabling him to win the ball cleanly and set the team off on an attack.

Jason is also able to operate at left-back but it is at centre-half where he is most comfortable, and it has been of little surprise to anyone at Carrow Road that he has taken his chance so positively.

After a series of impressive displays at the end of the 2004-05 season, a great deal is expected of Jason in the coming campaign.

STATS 2004-05	App	⚽	🟨	🟥
League	11	0	1	0
FA Cup	0	0	0	0
Carling Cup	1	0	0	0
Total	**12**	**0**	**1**	**0**

Damien **Francis**

Date of Birth February 27, 1979
Place of Birth Wandsworth
Previous Clubs Wimbledon
Norwich Debut August 9, 2003 vs Bradford City (A) 2-2
Total Norwich Appearances 76 (2)
Total Norwich Goals 14
Squad No 20

MIDFIELDER

STATS 2004-05				
	App	⚽	🟨	🟥
League	32	7	3	0
FA Cup	1	0	0	0
Carling Cup	2	0	0	0
Total	**35**	**7**	**3**	**0**

Damien Francis enjoyed a memorable first season at Carrow Road after joining the Club from Wimbledon in the summer of 2003.

A strong and athletic midfielder, Damien's box-to-box running and robust tackling skills have won him many admirers.

He took to the Barclays Premiership scene like a duck to water in the opening four months of the 2004-05 season, scoring four goals from midfield – including a brace as City recorded their first League win of the season over Southampton in November.

Sadly, a freak facial injury sustained after a training ground collision sidelined Damien until New Year's Day, when he returned to the side with a goal in City's 1-1 draw at Portsmouth.

Damien weighed in with two more goals in the second-half of the season, including a vital winner over West Bromwich Albion in February but his all round game never reached the dizzy heights that he produced in the opening months of the season.

With seven goals from midfield and a runner-up slot in the Player of the Year awards, 2004-05 was a great success for Damien Francis.

Player Profiles

Jason **Jarrett**

Date of Birth September 14, 1979
Place of Birth Bury
Previous Clubs Blackpool, Wrexham, Bury, Wigan Athletic, Stoke City (Loan)
Norwich Debut N/A
Total Norwich Appearances 0
Total Norwich Goals 0
Squad No 7

MIDFIELDER

STATS 2004-05				
	App	⚽	🟨	🟥
League	4 (10)	0	1	0
FA Cup	1	0	0	0
Carling Cup	0	0	0	0
Total	**5 (10)**	**0**	**1**	**0**

Jason Jarrett joined the Canaries on a Bosman-style free transfer in the summer of 2005 after rejecting the offer of a new three-year contract with Barclays Premiership new boys Wigan Athletic.

The 25-year-old midfielder will be reuniting with City boss Nigel Worthington after the pair worked together at Blackpool where Jason began his career during Nigel's time as manager at Bloomfield Road.

An athletic midfielder, Jason made his professional debut for the Seasiders before taking in spells at Wrexham and Bury. It was from Bury that he joined Wigan in March 2002 for a knockdown £75,000, with the Gigg Lane club desperate to boost their finances.

He made an immediate impact at Wigan and in his first full season helped the Latics to win the old Second Division championship in 2003. Jason enjoyed an impressive season at the JJB Stadium in 2003-04, but a broken leg sustained in pre-season ahead of the 2004-05 campaign saw him miss out on a majority of the Latics' promotion-winning season.

A loan spell at Stoke City helped him regain his fitness in the early part of 2005 before he returned to the Wigan squad for the end of season run-in.

With over 150 League appearances to his name, Jason brings a useful blend of youth and experience with him to Carrow Road. Tagged a box-to-box midfielder, Jason's arrival at Carrow Road will stiffen up competition for places in the Canary midfield as City build for the 2005-06 Coca-Cola Championship campaign.

Mattias **Jonson**

Date of Birth January 16, 1974
Place of Birth Orebro, Sweden
Previous Clubs Helsingborgs, Brondby
Norwich Debut August 14, 2004 vs Crystal Palace (H) 1-1
Total Norwich Appearances 21 (9)
Total Norwich Goals 0
Squad No 9

Sweden international Mattias Jonson joined the Canaries on the eve of the 2004-05 Barclays Premiership campaign.

The 31-year-old former FC Brondby man agreed a two-year deal with City and made his debut on the opening day of the season at home to Crystal Palace.

Comfortable on either flank, or even as a centre-forward, Mattias played in every one of his country's Euro 2004 games as the Swedish side progressed to the quarter-finals before going out to Holland on penalties.

A strong and pacy frontman, a lot was expected of Mattias upon his arrival at Carrow Road, but like so many foreign imports he struggled to make an impact during the Canaries' opening games of the season. He adjusted to the pace of the English game as the season progressed, however, and his commitment to the Canary cause – which was typified by playing on with a nasty head injury sustained against Liverpool – has seen him become a firm favourite with the fans.

MIDFIELDER

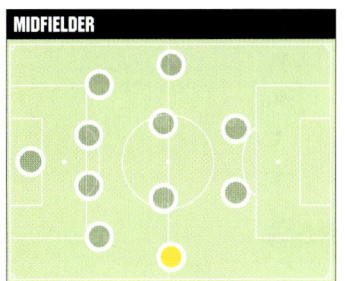

STATS 2004-05				
	App	⚽	🟨	🟥
League	19 (9)	0	2	1
FA Cup	1	0	0	0
Carling Cup	1	0	0	0
Total	**21 (9)**	**0**	**2**	**1**

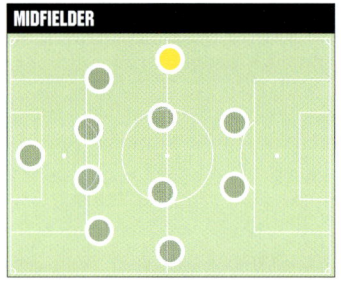

MIDFIELDER

Paul **McVeigh**

Date of Birth December 6, 1977
Place of Birth Belfast
Previous Clubs Tottenham Hotspur
Norwich Debut May 7, 2000 vs Bolton Wanderers (A) 0-1
Total Norwich Appearances 131 (41)
Total Norwich Goals 32
Squad No 18

Paul McVeigh began his career at Tottenham Hotspur and progressed through the youth and reserve team ranks before earning his first professional contract at White Hart Lane.

With his first-team opportunities being limited at the North London club, Paul opted to join the Canaries in March 2000.

Despite arriving at Norwich as a recognised striker, Paul has spent most of his time at Carrow Road in wide positions – mostly on the left, but occasionally operating in an unfamiliar role on the right side of midfield.

During his time with the Canaries, he has played 172 games and chipped in with an impressive haul of 32 goals.

Despite playing a major part in the Club's 2003-04 promotion-winning campaign, Paul rarely figured in 2004-05, starting just three Barclays Premiership games.

At the end of the season he was told by manager Nigel Worthington that he was available for transfer. His immediate future at the Club therefore remains unclear.

STATS 2004-05				
	App	⚽	🟨	🟥
League	3 (14)	1	0	0
FA Cup	0	0	0	0
Carling Cup	1	0	0	0
Total	4 (14)	1	0	0

Youssef **Safri**

Date of Birth January 3, 1977
Place of Birth Casablanca
Previous Clubs Raja Casablanca, Coventry City
Norwich Debut August 28, 2004 vs Arsenal (H) 1-4
Total Norwich Appearances 14 (6)
Total Norwich Goals 2
Squad No 15

MIDFIELDER

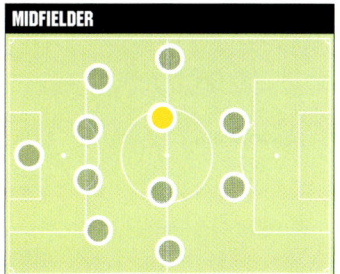

Morocco international midfielder Youssef Safri joined the Canaries in July 2004 from Coventry City for an initial fee of £500,000.

A tough-tackling yet creative midfielder, the 27-year-old signed a two-year deal at Carrow Road.

Youssef was a crowd favourite at Highfield Road after joining the Sky Blues from Raja Casablanca in August 2001.

He became an integral part of the Moroccan national side during his time with Coventry and played a major part in the African Cup of Nations campaign in 2004.

Youssef tends to adopt a shoot on sight policy, something that served him well as he scored his first goal for the Canaries during the Carling Cup success over Bristol Rovers in September 2004.

A series of niggling injuries interrupted his Canary career in the first half of the campaign, but he returned to the side for the thrilling end-of-season run.

His wonder-goal against Newcastle United will be talked about for years to come at Carrow Road.

STATS 2004-05	App	⚽	🟨	🟥
League	13 (5)	1	4	0
FA Cup	0	0	0	0
Carling Cup	1 (1)	1	0	0
Total	**14 (6)**	**2**	**4**	**0**

Player Profiles

STRIKER

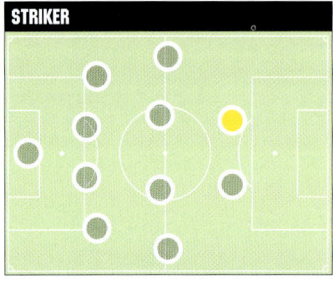

STATS 2004-05				
	App	⚽	🟨	🟥
League	16	7	0	0
FA Cup	0	0	0	0
Carling Cup	0	0	0	0
Total	**16**	**7**	**0**	**0**

Dean **Ashton**

Date of Birth November 24, 1983
Place of Birth Swindon
Previous Clubs Crewe Alexandra
Norwich Debut January 15, 2005 vs Aston Villa (A) 0-3
Total Norwich Appearances 16
Total Norwich Goals 7
Squad No 10

Dean Ashton became Norwich City's record signing when he joined the Canaries from Crewe Alexandra for a fee of £3million in January 2005.

A product of Dario Gradi's famed Crewe Academy, Dean joined the Gresty Road club as a schoolboy and went on to progress through the youth ranks to earn his first professional contract.

He made his League debut for Crewe in October 2000, coming on as a second-half substitute during a match at Gillingham. His first start then came in a FA Cup replay against Cardiff City in January 2001.

A first League goal came during Crewe's 4-2 home success over Burnley in February 2001, and regular first-team football followed.

The goals soon began to flow for Dean and his progress was constantly monitored by a number of Premier League scouts.

His goalscoring ability was rewarded with international recognition. He has been capped by England at various youth levels, including Under-19 and Under-21.

The 2004-05 season saw Dean top the Coca-Cola Championship scoring charts, and once the January transfer window opened Canary boss Nigel Worthington made Dean's signing his number one priority.

A powerful striker with great close control and a superb eye for goal, Dean had no problem taking his talents on to the Barclays Premiership stage and registered seven goals in 16 games for the Canaries.

Ian **Henderson**

STRIKER

Date of Birth January 24, 1985
Place of Birth Thetford
Previous Clubs N/A
Norwich Debut October 23, 2002 vs Coventry City (A) 1-1
Total Norwich Appearances 19 (28)
Total Norwich Goals 5
Squad No 22

Ian Henderson was the first player to come from the Club's Academy and play first team football for the Canaries when he made his debut away to Coventry in October 2002.

The young striker has great enthusiasm for the game and approaches all that he does on the pitch in a competitive manner.

He enjoyed a productive season during the Canaries' 2003-04 championship-winning campaign, starting 14 Nationwide First Division games and scoring four goals.

Frustratingly for Ian, his 2004-05 season was dogged by a series of niggling injuries and he was limited to just four substitute appearances for the first team.

Despite a lack of club action he continues to remain involved with England at Under-20 level, where he tends to play in his preferred role as a striker.

He was included in the England Under-20 squad for the Toulon Tournament and will be looking to use that as a springboard for a successful 2005-06 season at club level.

STATS 2004-05	App	⚽	🟨	🟥
League	0 (3)	0	0	0
FA Cup	0	0	0	0
Carling Cup	0 (1)	0	0	0
Total	**0 (4)**	**0**	**0**	**0**

Player Profiles

Darren **Huckerby**

Date of Birth April 23, 1976
Place of Birth Nottingham
Previous Clubs Lincoln City, Newcastle United, Millwall (Loan), Coventry City, Leeds United, Manchester City
Norwich Debut September 13, 2003 vs Burnley (H) 2-0
Total Norwich Appearances 76 (1)
Total Norwich Goals 21
Squad No 6

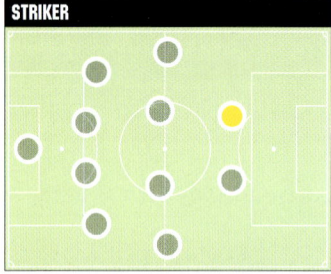

STRIKER

Darren Huckerby enjoyed yet another highly successful season with the Canaries, which ended with the jet-heeled striker landing the prestigious 2004-05 Player of the Year award.

Darren played in all but two of the Canaries' Barclays Premiership fixtures, scoring six goals and laying on countless others for his team-mates.

Whether employed as an out-and-out striker or drifting in from the left, Darren caused havoc among many Premiership defences last season. In fact, statistics confirmed he ended the campaign as the Premiership's most fouled player.

After joining the Canaries from Manchester City last season, Darren has turned in countless match-winning performances and has become a real crowd favourite at Carrow Road.

With an abundance of experience from spells with Lincoln City, Newcastle, Coventry, Leeds and Manchester City to call upon, Darren is viewed as one of the senior members of Nigel Worthington's squad, and the Carrow Road faithful will be looking for even more exciting performances from him in 2005-06.

STATS 2004-05

	App	⚽	🟨	🟥
League	36 (1)	6	0	0
FA Cup	1	0	0	0
Carling Cup	2	1	1	0
Total	39 (1)	7	1	0

Ryan **Jarvis**

Date of Birth July 11, 1986
Place of Birth Fakenham, Norfolk
Previous Clubs N/A
Norwich Debut April 19, 2003 vs Walsall (A) 0-0
Total Norwich Appearances 4 (18)
Total Norwich Goals 2
Squad No 23

Like Ian Henderson and Jason Shackell, Ryan Jarvis is another product of the Canaries' Academy set-up.

He made history when he became the Club's youngest-ever player after making his debut at Walsall on April 19, 2003 aged just 16 years, 282 days.

Despite bursting on to the scene over two years ago, Ryan may be a little frustrated that he has failed to make a first team place his own over the past two seasons.

An intelligent striker, Ryan has the ability to find both time and space, even in the most difficult situations.

Like a number of players at Carrow Road last season, Ryan's campaign wasn't helped by a couple of minor injury problems. He still managed four Barclays Premiership appearances and scored a wonderful long-range goal against Liverpool at Carrow Road in January.

Ryan ended the season with a loan spell at Coca-Cola League One club Colchester United and will really be looking to make a big impression at Carrow Road next season.

STRIKER

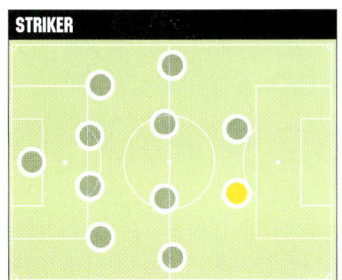

STATS 2004-05

	App	⚽	🟨	🟥
League	1 (3)	1	0	0
FA Cup	0 (1)	0	0	0
Carling Cup	0	0	0	0
Total	1 (4)	1	0	0

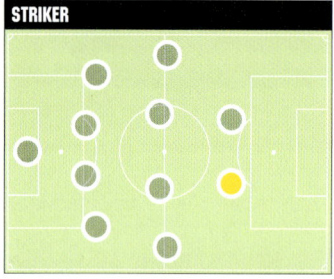

STRIKER

Leon **McKenzie**

Date of Birth May 17, 1978
Place of Birth Croydon
Previous Clubs Crystal Palace, Peterborough United
Norwich Debut December 21, 2004 vs Ipswich Town (A) 2-0
Total Norwich Appearances 36 (19)
Total Norwich Goals 16
Squad No 14

After marking his Canary debut with the two goals that handed the Canaries a memorable 2-0 derby day victory over arch-rivals Ipswich Town at Portman Road, Leon McKenzie's popularity at Carrow Road has continued to grow and grow.

A real all-action striker, Leon's passion for scoring goals has won him cult status amongst the Carrow Road faithful.

Few would believe that 18 months ago he was playing Second Division football with Peterborough United, such was the impression he made on the Barclays Premiership stage during 2004-05.

Together with Damien Francis, Darren Huckerby and Dean Ashton, Leon finished the season as the Canaries' joint-top scorer with seven goals.

Following the arrival of Ashton in January the two players soon formed a great understanding and it is that McKenzie, Huckerby, Ashton attack that so many Canary fans have high hopes for during the 2005-06 season.

STATS 2004-05	App	⚽	🟨	🟥
League	24 (13)	7	4	0
FA Cup	0	0	0	0
Carling Cup	0	0	0	0
Total	**24 (13)**	**7**	**4**	**0**

Peter **Thorne**

Date of Birth June 21, 1973
Place of Birth Manchester
Previous Clubs Blackburn Rovers, Wigan Athletic (Loan), Swindon Town, Stoke City, Cardiff City
Norwich Debut N/A
Total Norwich Appearances 0
Total Norwich Goals 0
Squad No 8

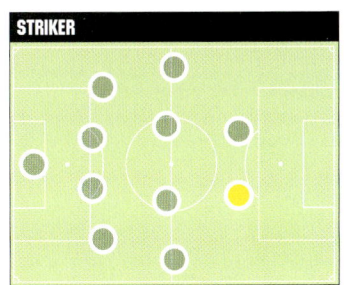

STRIKER

STATS 2004-05	App	⚽	🟨	🟥
League	28 (3)	12	0	0
FA Cup	1 (1)	0	0	0
Carling Cup	2	2	0	0
Total	**31 (4)**	**14**	**0**	**0**

Peter Thorne became Nigel Worthington's third summer signing when he was unveiled as a Norwich City player on Friday, July 1, 2005, alongside fellow new boys Jason Jarrett and Matthieu Louis-Jean.

A vastly experienced striker, Peter began his career with Blackburn Rovers and took in a loan spell at Wigan before leaving Ewood Park for Swindon Town in January 1995. It was at the County Ground that he made his name as an excellent leader of the line with a fantastic eye for goal, notching 27 League goals from just 78 League games. An equally impressive haul of 65 goals in 157 League games for Stoke City followed and resulted in Cardiff City recording their club-record signing when they paid the Potters £1.75million for Peter's services in September 2001.

His time in South Wales was again a successful one, with 46 goals from his 126 League outings for the Bluebirds.

Standing at 6ft, Peter is more than useful in the air as well as on the deck, and with a goals-to-games ratio that any striker would rightly be proud of, his arrival at Carrow Road on a free transfer has been seen as a major coup by City boss Nigel Worthington.

Goals make heroes and with such an impressive track record Peter Thorne looks set to be popular with all at Carrow Road.

Player of the Year

This was an award for a season and a bit. The defining moment for most Canary supporters in recent times was Norwich City's Christmas present of Darren to the fans in 2003, and I missed it being in San Francisco – and it wasn't even the baseball season! What was I thinking?

It's good to smile when everything goes wrong, but it's better to stop smiling and do something about it. Canary Chief Executive Neil Doncaster on a seemingly sad Tuesday said: "Darren will not be rejoining us."

So many twists and turns thereafter before Barry Skipper's and Nigel Worthington's perseverance to get "Hucks" paid off. We all learn from experience; no man wakes up his second baby just to see it smile. The "Hucks" second coming after a successful loan spell was the catalyst for promotion to the Premiership – it simply put the smile on faces.

> ## "It was a very emotional moment and I don't mind admitting there were a few tears in my eyes."
> ### Delia Smith

Here was a player of ripe experience – seven previous League clubs, played and scored in Europe and in different League and Cup competitions. Everyone knows he has electric pace, can play wide, off another player or up front on his own. Joe Royle, on signing him for Manchester City, said, "Our detective work has shown that he's a smashing lad who loves his training."

He lived a few doors away from David O'Leary (his daughter used to babysit for them) and the then Leeds United manager ventured: "A great lad to have around, but I had four other strikers in Viduka, Smith, Bridges and Keane."

Bill and Wendy are proud parents of their footballing sons Darren and Scott. The only downside for them is not seeing the Norwich branch of the family more often, as football has demands that do not ease until the summer break. There is superb sibling rivalry between the brothers in the nicest sense, with Darren being 16 months older and slightly taller. They both attended and played for Highbank Primary School, Fairham Community College, Clifton All Whites Youth Club, Pheasant Colts, Nottingham Boys, Nottinghamshire, Notts County and Lincoln City.

Darren, a Notts County fan, was rejected by them at 15 (told he wasn't big enough), so he went to a gym one hour away on a regular basis, such was his determination to succeed. My own first notice of Darren came before most people as I am acknowledged for assisting the brothers Nannested in their Who's Who of Lincoln City 1892-1994. Darren's professional contract at Sincil Bank of August 12, 1994 was followed by Scott's trainee signing for "The Imps" one month later. Incidentally at the club were Gary Megson and Jason Minett. By 60 League appearances Darren had worn nine different shirt numbers, supplemented years later by his donning the 'keeper's jersey in Alex Notman's testimonial match.

Scott, released by Lincoln in July 1996, embarked on a fine career in non-league football for 10 clubs, culminating in scoring the only goal for Arnold Town versus Eastwood Town in the 2005 Notts Senior Cup Final. A knee injury when with Telford United put his career on hold for nine months.

Darren has netted over 100 senior goals and Scott, unsure of his own total, says mischievously, "Add five to Darren's total and that's about right for me." Both are goalscorers on debuts, with Darren's being for Lincoln, Millwall, Manchester City and Nottingham Forest. Scott's starters were for Ilkeston Town, Hucknall Town, Kidsgrove Athletic and Grantham Town. Scott's three hat-tricks have been surpassed by Darren's five, plus a four-goal haul for Manchester City in a Worthington Cup

Player of the Year

slaughter of Birmingham. Only three Coventry players – Clarrie Boulton (1932), Arthur Bacon (1933-34) and George Lowrie (1947) – have matched Darren in scoring a hat-trick in successive games for the Club (Darren's 1999 efforts were against Macclesfield and Nottingham Forest). Arthur Bacon did, however, raise the bar to a new height, as his were a four and a five. (He was tragically killed during a 1942 air raid aged just 37.)

> **"I really have been surprised by how much our fans have taken to me – they've been brilliant. I think they appreciate the way I play, though I don't do things right all the time."**
>
> *Darren Huckerby*

What of the brothers' rivalry outside football? Scott, who works for Paul Smith, the clothes designer, says, "I have a healthy lead in pool games on Darren's own table." They were and both still are fine tennis players, with the eldest once resorting to a wrestling hold (not against Scott) on court.

What of the last Norwich City campaign? On-form Darren influences games. A highlight for me was the Highbury special from Darren, fittingly the 1,000th top-flight Norwich City goal and the only goal conceded by Arsenal in an 11-game spell. In a team effort what you do doesn't always count; it's what the other fellows do when you do what you do. Darren bamboozles opponents and creates chances in every game. His twisting, dazzling runs thrill the supporters.

Ability is a good thing, but stability – including a stable home life – is almost as important. He met wife Lyndsey when he was a trainee at Lincoln and they have two sons, Thomas and Ben.

Players past and present have had their say...

> **"We played Under-21's together, both called Darren, similar age and hairstyles – and I had mine done first."**
>
> Darren Eadie

> **"If I was playing I'd never get anywhere near him. I'd have to have a Suzuki bike to catch him. Fox and Ekoku were the closest we had and they weren't as quick as him."**
>
> Rob Newman

> **"I'm glad that I don't have to play against him."**
>
> Craig Fleming

> **"Darren was a worthy winner and one of the privileges of being chairman of this great Club is that I get to hand over the Player of the Season trophy. It was a magic moment for me."**
>
> Chairman Roger Munby, on presenting the Barry Butler Memorial Trophy

> **"I've got two seasons left on my contract and there's no doubt I'll be here for those two seasons. It doesn't matter who comes in, it won't interest me at all."**
>
> Darren Huckerby

Flying, Falling – Former first team players

Once again Norwich City historian Mike Davage provides us with an up-to-date run-down on the whereabouts and lives of a host of former Canaries.

Very pleasing to see that **Charles Abbs** will be featured in a forthcoming book about the 17th Middlesex Regiment, known as the *Footballers' Battalion*.

Zema Abbey, as devoted Canary followers will know, suffered damage to the anterior cruciate ligaments in both knees. Last season he played for four clubs – Boston United (with his brother Nathan), Bradford City, Wycombe Wanderers (with Clint Easton) and was finally released by Torquay United – it can be a transient life. I liked a newspaper article that said that **Neil Adams**, as an Everton player, breezed into a hotel foyer in Madrid asking for directions to the beach! He denied it in one of his syndicated columns in the local press. **Ade Akinbiyi** netted goals for his new club Burnley. A sad and proud day for **Terry Allcock** was his being the funeral director for the late Geoffrey Watling. I shall miss the latter's Christmas cards. **Malcolm Allen** was highlighted in a Spurs programme as being their Under-15 academy coach. **Cedric Anselin** is difficult to track – he's had trials, looked at the town and played some games since the last yearbook for Cambridge United, Ionikos (Piraeus), Southend United, Gravesend & Northfleet, and Norwich United. I make that 15 clubs and he's only 28. **Dean Ashton** is Norwich City's 671st Football League player. As a youngster he followed Manchester United; his most ever goals in a match was six when at school and he acquired a 4.4 BMW (previously had a Porsche) because it's better for his hamstrings. He'll go far in the beautiful game. William Leslie became **William Leslie Askew** when his mother Jessie married a Liverpudlian stained glass artist. By the age of 35 she had seven children and frustratingly I still cannot find the demise of our most elusive player. Former England player **"Sam" Austin** prolonged his career with Shirley Town and post-war (when aged 47) as a permit player with Brinton's FC in the Kidderminster League.

Former goalkeeper **Clive Baker** once scored 187 for Cromer CC which included 12(6) and 17(4) – typical goalie, restrict the running! **Steve Ball** was appointed Clacton's assistant manager in the Ridgeons League. **Craig Bellamy** scored vital goals while on loan to Glasgow Celtic and was man of the match in his club's Scottish Cup Final win over Dundee United. A marvelous letter arrived from Edith Thwaites who fondly recalled her uncle **Walter Bell,** known as "Dinger": "I don't remember the players hugging and cuddling each other half as much," she said. **Trevor Benjamin** is another traveller and added to his CV are clubs Rotherham United, Northampton Town and Coventry City. Thanks to **David Bentley** who gave us glimpses of his undoubted ability. **Kevin Bond** couldn't save my home town club Southampton from relegation, but he moved up to the post of assistant manager. **Jimmy Bone** became the Partick Thistle assistant manager last January. **Mark Bowen** left Birmingham to become Blackburn Rovers assistant manager to Mark Hughes. **Keith Briggs**

Neil Adams

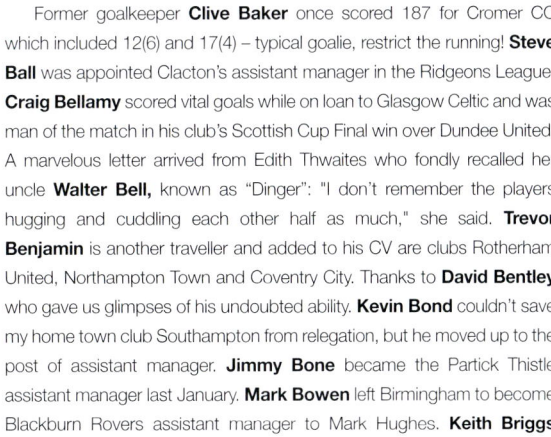

Craig Bellamy

last season had trials, training sessions and/or loans with Crewe, Sheffield United, Gillingham and Wycombe before signing for Stockport County. **Leigh Bromby** joined Sheffield United. **Drewe Broughton** made another appearance at the Millennium Stadium for Southend United after loan spells at Rushden & Diamonds (netted a hat-trick versus Notts County) and Wycombe Wanderers. The Spanish "Roundtown News" edition 252 gave the exclusive that having overturned an outdated and unfair law whereby foreign European nationals were not allowed to play in the Valencian Leagues, the club FC Torrevieja were to sign **Kenny Brown.** Newcastle United held a reunion for the class of '69 in April 2005, with former Norwich City player **Ollie Burton** being an attendee. **Viv Busby** had a spell as caretaker manager at York City. **Geoff Butler** as the Rymans League Division One Bashley's manager gave an excellent interview in the local paper prior to City's match against champions Chelsea.

Shaun Carey joined Hornchurch in the Ryman League. **Johnny Church** sadly passed away in Carlton Colville on September 6, 2004 just 11 days short of his 85th birthday. A grand innings for a remarkable man. **Dean Coney** accepted the appointment as Redbridge FC's assistant manager last January. **Kevin Cooper** was put on Wolverhampton Wanderers' transfer list.

Adrian Coote joined Dereham Town (scored a hat-trick) and also netted both goals for Gorleston Feathers as they won the Norfolk Sunday Intermediate Cup. Damian Hilton, the latest Wroxham manager, has just signed him for his club. Three-times Manchester City Supporters Player of the Year **Joe Corrigan** has been the goalkeeping coach at Chester, Liverpool, Stockport County and W.B.A. **Paul Crichton** has seen action with York City, Stafford Rangers, Leigh RMI and Accrington Stanley since July 2004. **Ian Crook** is the assistant coach at Australia's Sydney FC. **David Cross** is part of the academy set-up at Blackburn Rovers. **Peter Crouch** has aspired to the lofty heights of being an England player. **Danny Crow** scored goals for Northampton Town under the guidance of their director of football John Deehan. **Ian Culverhouse** was a casualty last May in a backroom reshuffle at Leyton Orient. **Jamie Cureton** was released by QPR and he returned to Carrow Road for Alex Notman's testimonial match.

Are there any experts out there who can help find the whereabouts of our former goalkeeper of yesteryear **John Denoon**? **John Devine** owns a furniture business in Dublin and also runs the Manchester United youth academy in Ireland. **Louie Donowa**, a driver in Tamworth, missed the Norwich City Milk Cup reunion at Carrow Road. **Adam Drury**, incidentally, won the 2005 Norwich City premier golf classic.

Bob Edwards had one game in Chelsea's First Division Championship-winning season. We wish **Marc Edworthy** well after his release – he was last seen by the author at Elton John's Carrow Road concert. I was pleased to be involved in having the brother of our 1903 player **Horace Ellis**, namely Ernie, being commemorated in a fine book,

Neil Emblen

Peter Crouch

Flying, Falling – Former first team players

McCrae's Battalion, the story of the 16th Royal Scots during WWI. **Neil Emblen** headed across the globe to join Auckland based New Zealand Knights in the Australian A League. Our former towering goalkeeper **George Ephgrave** died in Guernsey on December 9, 2004 age 86. **Robert Fleck** was viewed on Sky TV playing in the European Indoor Masters (in Paisley) for a triumphant Glasgow Rangers who overcame Ajax in the final. He also played in the Diss Town vs Norwich All Stars match in May 2005 to raise money for a Norfolk Tsunami victims fund. "The All Stars are all good players in their own right. Nowadays kids don't tend to know us, but the parents do," said Fleck. A busy season saw Robert lead Diss Town to reclaiming the Norfolk Senior Cup at Carrow Road last May. **Adrian Forbes** scored the only goal to finally secure Swansea's automatic promotion. The Montserrat international **Ruel Fox** scored on his debut versus Antigua when aged 36. He credits Rob Newman for kindling his interest in management and coaching in letting him train and coach at Southend United. Ruel took on the role as manager of Whitton United in Ipswich.

Dale Gordon played in the same tournament as Robert Fleck for Glasgow Rangers. **Jeremy Goss** netted for the Norwich All Stars last April in a fundraising match against Diss Town at Brewers Green Lane, with **Bryan Gunn** missing a penalty in the same match. **Elvis Hammond** joined Dutch side RBC Roosendaal. **Kevin Harper**, since leaving Norwich City, has had a loan spell with Leicester City before signing for Stoke City in a 30-month deal. I am investigating whether our 1903 half-back **Edward Harris** did in fact pass away in 1947. **Asa Hartford** was replaced at Manchester City by Steve Wigley. **David Healy** joined Leeds United last October. **Paul Heckingbottom** played for Sheffield Wednesday and Bradford City last season. **Scott Howie** was released by Shrewsbury Town. Norwich City's half-back signing in July 1908 was **Harry Bonthron Hutchison** born Carstairs, County of Lanark on March 25, 1883. His father Thomas was a locomotive stoker who married Elizabeth Bonthron on Xmas Eve 1878. Now to find his demise.

Hearty congratulations to **Matt Jackson** for helping his Wigan side to promotion. Our 1950's winger **Denys Jones** died May 4, 2003. I must do a feature on the marvelous Jennings brothers of the 1920's era plus the Lamberton's of over a decade before. The resplendent **Sandy Kennon** was part of a Canary trio that entertained Yarmouth Town FC on a "soccer chat night" last May. **Darren Kenton** was loaned to Leicester City, but he returned to Southampton for a spell to recover from mumps. **Andy Linighan** swapped his football boots and shin pads for a length of copper piping and a monkey wrench and in an Evening News feature last April was hopeful that Norwich City would stay up. **Chris Llewellyn's** Wrexham side were relegated, ultimately being unable to claw back the 10 points deducted for going into administration.

Brian McGovern joined Shamrock Rovers on loan last march. Our best wishes to **Phil Mulryne**, who was released by mutual consent.

Adrian Forbes

Chris Llewellyn

Flying, Falling – Former first team players

Ted MacDougall is the Program (American spelling) Director for boys at Tucker Youth Soccer Academy in Atlanta and is the proud owner of a USSFA National License. **Malky Mackay** barnstormed with West Ham United. **Lee Marshall** retired through injury last April. **Gary Megson** could not save Nottingham Forest from relegation. **Ian Mellor's** son Neil scored a semi-final goal for Liverpool in the Worthington Cup. **Jason Minett** joined Lincoln United. **Neil Moore** moved to Stafford Rangers.

Steen Nedergaard announced that he was moving to Hvidovre. **Rob Newman** is a busy boy. He scouts for Birmingham, assists with training and occasionally plays for Gorleston, and became the Cambridge United caretaker manager last May. **Jon Newsome** was plying his trade at Spalding United. **David Nielsen** had problems at Aalborg, so he joined FC Midtyylland in the Danish Premier Division. Did you know **Maurice Norman** was due to play golf with the legendary John White (Spurs) but decided against it because of the bad weather? John played and was killed when lightning struck his ring finger. **Alex Notman** was graciously granted a benefit match following his enforced retirement.

Keith O'Neill had a successful benefit dinner in Dublin last May with footballers, snooker stars and entertainment celebrities among the invitees. It was all our yesterdays as he scored a memorable goal at Portman Road against an Ipswich Town select side for Sky TV's "The Badgers". **Martin O'Neill's** Celtic won another trophy, but for once in recent times Rangers pipped them to the title. A Scottish Cup Final victory was his last game in charge as he resigned for personal reasons. I am finally closing in on Private **Andrew Muir Osborne** of the 16th Lancers. **Peter Osgood** said that he was going to have a party in the Kings Road following Chelsea's Premiership title.

Scott Parker struggled to force his way into Chelsea's multinational side and he is the subject of transfer speculation as we go to press. **Adrian Pennock** became the first team manager at Welling United. **Paul Peschiselido** netted twice versus Norwich City reserves last March. **Spencer Prior** played at the Millennium Stadium for Southend United.

Peter Rattray's widow Cathleen wrote a lovely letter explaining that her husband died on December 5, 2004 in Stirling Royal Infirmary after spending many years in hospital. Sadly missed by his two daughters, a son and three grandchildren. **Kevin Reeves** has upset me by scouting in the North and the Midlands for Portsmouth. **Mark Rivers** found his way back to Crewe after going on a pre season tour to Denmark with Ipswich Town. **Iwan Roberts** at Gillingham was their player coach and joint caretaker manager before arriving at Cambridge United. **Mark Robins** endured a third operation on his right knee and he resurfaced training with Burton Albion before joining Rotherham United's management team last January. The almost irreplaceable **Bernard Robinson** passed away last November age 92. He was my chosen guest, of all the available players, to accompany me to Carrow Road's Directors' Box at the launch of the 1986 "Canary Citizens". RIP, great man. Also sadly, **Brian Ronson**

Spencer Prior

Mark Robins

Flying, Falling – Former first team players

passed away unheralded and unnoticed in his home town in June 2003. **Gary Rowell** gave a fine interview to Evening News reporter Rick Waghorn last January highlighting his role in the media. **Joe Royle** became one of the few present-day men to have been a manager for 1,000 games.

Youssef Safri, Norwich City's first Moroccan player, was Coventry's third such acquisition and the 52nd overseas player for the Sky Blues in the Football League. **Fred Sharpe** revealed a nickname of "Iron Man" after one four-game spell in which he dislocated his shoulder, broke his nose and had stitches in a head wound above his eye but still played on in each occasion. One for Gary Holt in that Fred was called up for National Service in the Army Catering Corp but he never did any cooking. He spent most of his time training and playing football, as among his unit at Aldershot were Charlie Hurley, Dave Dunmore and Gerry Ward. Injury-plagued **Tim Sherwood** was made available on a free transfer by Coventry City. **Mike Sheron** was released by Shrewsbury Town last May. **Dean Sinclair**, released in 2004, trained and played a reserve game for Wimbledon before joining and starring for Barnet as they won elevation to the Football League. He also played for an England National XI at non-league level. **Tony Spearing** played some friendlies for Norwich United and joined Wisbech Town for a short time. **Henry Spinks** passed away in the Norfolk & Norwich University Hospital on February 18, 2005. A retired transport manager for Norwich City council, he is mourned by his widow, son, daughter and four grandchildren. **Billy Steele** is the Toronto Lynx (Canada) assistant manager. **Robert Whyte Stewart** was the son of Walter (a tailor journeyman) and he died on September 17, 1950 in Paisley aged just 50. Best wishes to **Graham Stuart**, who superbly answered my probing questions when he joined Norwich City. **Daryl Sutch** surfaced at Southend United and Wroxham, and also played in Alex Notman's bene-fit match at Carrow Road. **Chris Sutton** was a joy to behold with his Beckhamesque penalty miss in the Scottish Cup Final.

Maurice Tobin celebrated his 84th birthday and such is the affection for him Maurice Norman and John Wilson were surprise guests. They were both A team players under the guidance of Maurice and both related that Mr Tobin always tried to help the men become better players. **Robert Ullathorne** transferred to Notts County. **Dennis Van Wijk** came back to Carrow Road for the Milk Cup 20th anniversary reunion dinner. **Steve Walford** left Celtic in May 2005 along with Martin O'Neill. **Mark Walton** had a short time with Australian side Bentleigh Green in the Victoria Premier League. **Ashley Ward's** wife Dawn was featured in a national paper as an interior designer who is working on Wayne Rooney's Prestbury mansion. Ashley has been released by Sheffield United. **Dave Watson** is the Liverpool Schools Under-14 coach and he was another welcome attendee at the Milk Cup reunion. **Colin Woodthorpe** was released by Bury last May.

Tim Sherwood

Colin Woodthorpe

Reserves and Academy

Reserves

		P	Home					Away					GD	Pts
			W	D	L	F	A	W	D	L	F	A		
1	Charlton Athletic	28	11	2	1	29	9	7	5	2	17	12	+25	61
2	Southampton	28	11	2	1	39	13	7	2	5	29	16	+39	58
3	Arsenal	28	11	2	1	36	14	6	3	5	29	24	+27	56
4	Crystal Palace	28	8	4	2	25	9	8	1	5	22	13	+25	53
5	Tottenham	28	8	4	2	28	19	5	4	5	19	16	+12	47
6	Chelsea	28	5	6	3	11	10	5	2	7	17	18	0	38
7	Watford	28	7	2	5	18	13	2	7	5	14	20	-1	36
8	**Norwich City**	**28**	**5**	**2**	**7**	**9**	**12**	**5**	**2**	**7**	**15**	**28**	**-16**	**34**
9	Fulham	28	6	3	5	15	15	2	6	6	14	20	-6	33
10	Derby County	28	5	4	5	13	18	4	2	8	16	30	-19	33
11	West Ham	28	4	5	5	18	28	3	4	7	15	23	-18	30
12	Coventry City	28	4	4	6	18	27	3	4	7	11	23	-21	29
13	Ipswich Town	28	4	3	7	14	14	2	3	9	10	21	-11	24
14	Leicester City	28	2	5	7	23	30	3	4	7	13	19	-13	24
15	Portsmouth	28	4	4	6	19	19	1	3	10	9	32	-23	22

Reserves

RESERVE RESULTS – 2004-05

Date	Opponents	Result
Aug 18	West Ham United	1-2
Aug 23	Leicester City	3-3
Sep 1	Coventry City	1-3
Sep 8	Portsmouth	1-0
Sep 13	Chelsea	2-0
Sep 20	Tottenham Hotspur	0-2
Sep 29	Fulham	4-0
Oct 11	Ipswich Town	2-1
Oct 20	Crystal Palace	0-1
Oct 27	Watford	1-0
Nov 10	Southampton	1-0
Nov 15	Charlton Athletic	0-5
Nov 22	Arsenal	2-1
Dec 1	West Ham United	0-2
Dec 6	Leicester City	0-1
Dec 13	Coventry City	3-0
Jan 19	Chelsea	0-1
Jan 26	Tottenham Hotspur	0-2
Jan 31	Derby County	0-3
Feb 9	Fulham	0-1
Mar 1	Crystal Palace	1-0
Mar 9	Watford	1-0
Mar 15	Southampton	0-5
Mar 24	Derby County	0-2
Mar 30	Charlton Athletic	0-0
Apr 4	Arsenal	0-4
Apr 27	Ipswich Town	0-0
May 3	Portsmouth	1-1

RESERVE GOALSCORERS – 2004-05

NORTH

1	Moore	Aston Villa	18
2	Wright-Phillips	Manchester City	17
3	Rossi	Manchester United	16
4	Graham	Middlesbrough	15
5	Clarke	Wolverhampton W.	13
6	Vaz Te	Bolton Wanderers	11
=	Ebanks-Blake	Manchester United	11
7	Elvins	West Brom	10
8	Negouai	Manchester City	9
=	Kyle	Sunderland	9
9	Miller	Manchester City	8
10	Vaughan	Everton	7
=	Mellor	Liverpool	7
=	Jones	Manchester United	7
=	Bridges	Sunderland	7

SOUTH

1	Lupoli	Arsenal	19
2	Barnard	Tottenham	17
3	Best	Southampton	13
4	Junior	Derby County	10
5	Keene	Portsmouth	9
6	Aliadiere	Arsenal	8
=	Stokes	Arsenal	8
=	Sam	Charlton Athletic	8
7	Freedman	Crystal Palace	7
=	Crow	Norwich City	7
=	Blackstock	Southampton	7
=	Ashikodi	West Ham United	7
=	Rebrov	West Ham United	7

Reserves

Name	Appearances	Goals	Name	Appearances	Goals
Abbey	0 (1)	0	Holt	2	0
Asprey	0 (2)	0	Howell	3 (6)	0
Bentley	2	0	Howlett	9 (7)	1
Blackburn	12 (3)	0	Jarvis, Rossi	11 (4)	0
Brennan	17	0	Jarvis, Ryan	16 (1)	7
Briggs	1	0	Jonson	3	1
Bunn	0 (2)	0	Lacey	1	0
Cave Brown	13 (3)	0	Lewis	6	0
Charlton	6	0	McKenzie	4	2
Crow	17 (4)	7	McVeigh	15	1
Doherty	6	0	Mackay	1	0
Drury	1	0	Manning	1 (2)	0
Eagle	10 (5)	0	Martin	0 (2)	0
Edworthy	2	0	Mulryne	12	2
El Ouargui	2 (1)	0	Safri	8	0
Fisk	3 (1)	0	Shackell	15	0
Gallacher	12	0	Smith, A	16 (1)	1
Greenwood	1 (2)	0	Smith, L	2 (1)	0
Gusterson	8 (2)	0	Spillane	0 (3)	0
Halliday	21	0	Squire	1 (1)	0
Helveg	2	0	Svensson	6	0
Henderson	17	1	Ward	9	0
Herbert	1 (1)	0	Willis	13 (6)	0
Hill	0 (1)	0	Own goals	–	1

Academy

ACADEMY RESULTS – 2004-05

Date	Opponent	Result
Aug 21	Leeds United	1-4
Aug 27	Huddersfield Town	0-2
Sep 4	Tottenham Hotspur	2-2
Sep 11	Watford	2-0
Sep 18	MK Dons	4-2
Sep 25	Aston Villa	0-3
Oct 2	Arsenal	1-2
Oct 9	Fulham	0-0
Oct 16	Millwall	0-1
Oct 23	West Ham United	2-3
Oct 30	Chelsea	1-4
Nov 6	Charlton Athletic	0-1
Nov 13	Southampton	1-2
Nov 20	Ipswich Town	1-1
Dec 4	Crystal Palace	0-1
Dec 11	West Ham United	0-0
Dec 15	Burnley (FA Youth Cup)	2-1
Jan 8	Chelsea	1-0
Jan 14	Charlton Athletic	1-1
Jan 19	Southampton (FA Youth Cup)	0-1
Jan 22	Southampton	1-2
Feb 5	Ipswich Town	0-1
Feb 12	Crystal Palace	2-0
Feb 18	Arsenal	1-1
Mar 12	Millwall	1-0
Apr 2	Birmingham City	1-2
Apr 9	Bristol City	2-0
Apr 16	Cardiff City	1-1
Apr 23	Coventry City	0-1
Apr 30	Fulham	0-1

ACADEMY APPEARANCES – 2004-05

	League App	League ⚽	Youth Cup App	Youth Cup ⚽
Bell	2 (1)	0	0	0
Bexfield	6 (1)	0	1	0
Blackburn	9 (4)	0	0	0
Cave-Brown	26	0	2	0
Crow	6 (2)	4	0	0
Daley	0	0	0 (1)	0
Eagle	27	3	2	0
Eames	1	0	0	0
El Ouargui	5 (2)	1	1 (1)	1
Fisk	12 (3)	0	0	0
Gusterson	22 (1)	2	1	0
Halliday	23 (5)	0	2	0
Herbert	13	0	0	0
Howell, A	0	0	0 (1)	0
Howell, N	18 (2)	1	0	0
Howlett	19 (3)	0	2	0
Jarvis, Ro.	25 (1)	2	2	0
Jarvis, Ry.	1	0	0	0
Lewis	15 (1)	0	2	0
Martin	21 (5)	8	2	1
Muddel	11 (3)	1	2	0
Osborne	4 (1)	0	0	0
Paterson	0 (1)	0	0	0
Smart	6	3	1	0
Smith	9 (4)	0	0	0
Spillane	16 (4)	0	2	0
Willis	11 (5)	1	0	0

Fixture List 2005-06

Date	Team	Date	Team
Aug 6	**COVENTRY CITY**	Dec 31	Leicester City
Aug 9	**CREWE ALEXANDRA**	**Jan 2**	**PRESTON NORTH END**
Aug 13	**CRYSTAL PALACE**	Jan 7	FA CUP 3
Aug 20	Southampton	Jan 10/11	Carling Cup SF 1
Aug 23	MK Dons (Carling Cup 1)	Jan 14	Plymouth Argyle
Aug 27	**LEEDS UNITED**	**Jan 21**	**WATFORD**
Aug 29	Stoke City	Jan 24/25	Carling Cup SF 2
Sep 10	**PLYMOUTH ARGYLE**	Jan 28	FA CUP 4
Sep 13	Watford	Jan 31	Reading
Sep 18	Ipswich Town	**Feb 5**	**IPSWICH TOWN**
Sep 20/21	Carling Cup 2	Feb 11	Hull City
Sep 24	**READING**	**Feb 14**	**BRIGHTON & HOVE ALBION**
Sep 27	**HULL CITY**	**Feb 18**	**DERBY COUNTY** or FA CUP 5
Oct 1	Brighton & Hove Albion	Feb 25	Crystal Palace
Oct 15	**MILLWALL**	Feb 26	Carling Cup Final
Oct 18	Luton Town	**Mar 4**	**STOKE CITY**
Oct 22	Queens Park Rangers	Mar 11	Leeds United
Oct 25/26	Carling Cup 3	**Mar 18**	**SHEFFIELD UNITED**
Oct 29	**SHEFFIELD WEDNESDAY**	Mar 22	FA CUP 6
Nov 1	**CARDIFF CITY**	Mar 25	Burnley
Nov 5	Wolves	**Apr 1**	**LEICESTER CITY**
Nov 19	**LUTON TOWN**	Apr 8	Preston North End
Nov 22	Millwall	Apr 15	Sheffield Wednesday
Nov 26	Coventry City	**Apr 17**	**QUEENS PARK RANGERS**
Nov 29/30	Carling Cup 4	Apr 22	Cardiff City
Dec 3	Derby County	Apr 23	FA CUP SF
Dec 10	Crewe Alexandra	**Apr 30**	**WOLVES**
Dec 17	**SOUTHAMPTON**	May 6	Play-Off SF 1
Dec 20/21	Carling Cup 5	May 10	Play-Off SF 2
Dec 26	Sheffield United	May 13	FA CUP FINAL
Dec 28	**BURNLEY**	May 21	Play-Off Final

HOME FIXTURES IN BOLD. ALL FIXTURES ARE SUBJECT TO CHANGE.